THE MEANING AND MESSAGE OF LENT

The

Meaning and Message
of Lent

EUGENE R. FAIRWEATHER

HARPER & BROTHERS, PUBLISHERS
NEW YORK

Unless otherwise indicated, all New Testament quotations are from the E. J. Goodspeed translation in *The Complete Bible, An American Translation* (University of Chicago Press, 1939), copyright 1939 by the University of Chicago. Used by permission of the publisher.

Quotations from the Psalms are taken from "The Psalter" in *The Book of Common Prayer* of the Protestant Episcopal Church in the United States of America.

All other Old Testament quotations are from the English Revised Version (1885), herein abbreviated ERV.

To my mother, Lulu Rathbone Fairweather, and to the memory of my grandparents, Charles and Edna Rathbone

CONTENTS

INTRODUCTION   *A Lenten Book About Lent*   9

PART ONE   *GOOD NEWS*

Chapter 1   *The Human Mystery of Life and Death*   17

Chapter 2   *The Divine Mystery of Death and Resurrection*   37

Chapter 3   *Anticipation: The Red Sea*   53

PART TWO   *SACRED SIGNS*

Chapter 4   *Initiation: Baptism*   71

Chapter 5   *Representation: Holy Communion*   83

PART THREE   *SACRED SEASONS*

Chapter 6   *Commemoration: Sunday*   103

Chapter 7   *Celebration: Easter*   109

Chapter 8   *Preparation: Lent*   114

Chapter 9   *Concentration: Fasting*   120

Chapter 10   *Illumination: Instruction*   127

Chapter 11   *Restoration: Penitence*   135

PART FOUR   *VICTORS*

Chapter 12   *Imitation: The Martyrs*   145

Chapter 13   *Thanks Be to God!*   153

SOURCES   157

INTRODUCTION

A LENTEN BOOK ABOUT LENT

Lent is meant to be a time of intensive training in Christianity. We may think that the Victorian undergraduate who draped his room with black velvet for the Lenten season was extravagant and a bit of a show-off, but he did make one good point. Lent should be an atmosphere that surrounds us, an experience that gets into our flesh and nerves and bones, a way of life—not just a time when we give up a luxury or two and attend a few extra church services.

Of course, Christians have kept Lent very variously in different times and places, and our Lenten rules must always be adapted to our circumstances. It is obvious, for instance, that in the urban, religiously mixed society of the modern West we cannot concentrate on Lent in the way that a simpler society made up of practicing Christians would regard as quite normal. But most Christians could plunge into Lent much more enthusiastically than they do; very few of us really give its spirit a fair chance to touch and penetrate our lives. It may well be that our failure is not altogether our fault—perhaps no one has ever made clear to us the special meaning and definite purpose of Lent—but unquestionably we do fail.

One accepted way of keeping Lent is to read books about Christian faith and life. As long ago as the sixth century, St. Benedict in his Rule for monks specified that books were to be given out to all the brethren at the beginning of Lent—not, he made it plain, for browsing or skimming, but for serious, continuous reading. The idea seems sound, not least in the twentieth century when overwhelming streams of casual reading matter pour from the press. To settle down to six weeks of hard reading and thinking about our religion would by itself make Lent different from the rest of the year for most of us.

Our Lenten reading may suitably touch on any aspect of Christian doctrine and practice. What really matters is that we should seriously fix our attention on the truths of our faith and on our fitting response to those truths. But perhaps there is a special value in concentrating on the root meaning of Lent itself as a time-honored part of the experience of Christian living—particularly if I am right in thinking that a good many Christians are rather vague about the exact significance of their Lenten observance. At any rate, this Lenten book is going to stay very close to the central themes of Lent.

Certain themes belong especially to Lent because of the way it came into existence as a Christian institution. Lent is not merely an historical accident, a kind of spiritual tonic conventionally prescribed for the spring season. It has its own proper place in the Christian calendar and its own special relation to the Christian Gospel. The Lenten observance is linked to the solemn and joyful proclamation of the very heart of the Gospel in the Easter festival. The supreme fact of Christianity, to which Easter testifies, is the death and resurrection of Jesus Christ, and Lent is designed to help Christians grow closer to that fact. Lent began as a preparation of the whole Church for the Easter celebration of Christ's death and resurrection, with its remembrance of God's mighty deed in the past and its expectation of his crowning act in the future. Soon Lent came to include the preparation of converts to the Christian Church and faith for their Baptism at Easter, and this feature contributed a good deal to its development as a Christian institution. Before long it also incorporated the final preparation of penitents under discipline for their return to full fellowship just before Easter. As it developed, Lent obviously became a big and complex enterprise, yet we can easily see that it never lost its essential orientation toward the Paschal feast of the death and resurrection of the Son of God.

Granted that the root meaning of Lent is fixed by its unbreakable links with the Easter festival and all that it stands for, we could still select for our study any one of several aspects of the historical content of Lent and Easter. For example, we might take the great Gospel theme of death and resurrection and try to think ourselves a little way into the inexhaustible mystery of our salvation through Jesus Christ, crucified and risen. We might try to spell out the spiritual meaning of Baptism and to see how Lent, Easter, and Baptism are intimately connected both in theological idea and in historical fact, so that each sheds some light on the other two. Or we might take a long look at one of the traditional disciplines of Lent, such as the practice of fasting and abstinence. This book, however, has been planned as a sketch of the whole subject, rather than as a detailed study of a particular area. It provides nothing more ambitious than an outline of the various elements—Gospel truths, Gospel sacraments, historic Christian institutions and disciplines—that make up Lent and determine its meaning.

The cornerstone of Lent is the climactic truth of the Gospel, the good news of the divine victory in the dying and the rising again of Jesus Christ. Lent exists to make this story more real to our minds and hearts and more powerful in our lives. Our first concern, then, must be to get at the meaning of the Gospel itself. I intend to tackle this question in three stages. First, since the Church presents the Gospel to the world as good news for real men, I want to examine the human situation which the Gospel presupposes, the human experience of life and death into which God entered in Jesus Christ. Then, having found out something of the depth and urgency of the question of death for human beings, we shall be ready to look at what God has done to meet the ultimate threat of death. Finally, guided by the profound symbolism of the ancient Christian liturgies, we can go on to see how the Gospel of Christ is related to the wider story of God's mighty works in human history and in creation itself. In these various ways we may hope to gain some understanding both of man's real situation and of God's real action in human history.

The God of Christian faith, who has acted in history to bring life to dying mankind, has appointed certain sacred signs to bring men into vital contact with the reality of the Gospel. The most important of the signs are the "sacraments of the Gospel"; Holy Baptism and the Holy Communion or Eucharist. As we shall see, Baptism is the basis and the Eucharist the constant support of a Christian life lived according to the Gospel. If Lent is intended to aid our growth in the truth of the Gospel, it seems to follow that part of its purpose is to help us approach the sacraments of the Gospel with fuller understanding and deeper devotion. For that reason I propose to devote two chapters to Baptism and the Eucharist as signs and instruments of God's life-giving grace.

We come at last to Lent itself. From the first century onward, the Church has enshrined the sacraments of the Gospel in the rich setting of the liturgical year, with Sunday and Easter, the Sunday of Sundays, as its basic components. The great cycle of the Christian year is one of the chief historic expressions of the common Christian understanding of the Gospel, and Lent, as preparation for the "royal Feast of feasts," is one of its most august and meaningful features. We shall first look at Sunday and Easter, as the foundation of the Christian year, and then go on to consider the origin and the meaning of Lent, with some attention to each aspect of the traditional Lenten discipline.

The truth of the Gospel, which is the meaning of the sacraments and the message of Lent and Easter, is a real-life story for real people and produces real results in human lives. The liturgical year, which bears witness to the Gospel itself, testifies also to the effects of the Gospel in the lives and deaths of the saints. On the great cycle, which runs from Sunday to Sunday and from Easter to Easter, the Church has superimposed another pattern, made up of the festivals of martyrs and other heroes of the faith. There is no better way to find out what the Gospel should mean in our lives than to see how it has brought love and hope and courage into countless Christian lives before us. Our final task will be to see how the Gospel of Lent and Easter has been published in the flesh and blood of the martyrs, and how it is our Christian calling to set forth the same Gospel in our own living and dying.

The roots of Lent in the Gospel of Jesus Christ, crucified and risen, and in the sacraments of the Gospel; the setting of Lent in the noble structure of the Christian calendar of worship and devotion; the demand of the Lenten message on our life and death—these are great and mysterious themes that Lent forces on our attention. In a brief treatment such as this we can barely begin to take due account of them. But the themes themselves have a strange power to attract and inspire, and it may be that even a hurried glance will encourage some readers to come just a little closer to the tremendous reality of which Lent speaks.

PART ONE
GOOD NEWS

CHAPTER 1

THE HUMAN MYSTERY OF LIFE AND DEATH

Dear, beauteous death! the Jewel of the Just,
　Shining nowhere, but in the dark;
What mysteries do lie beyond thy dust;
　Could man outlook that mark!
　　　　　　—Henry Vaughan

I

Man, the old definition says, is a rational animal. One could use more words and end up with a less convincing account of what we know ourselves to be. That man is a living organism, closely related to other creatures of the sort we call "animals," is beyond question. That man is rational, in any very strong sense of the word, may seem less evident to any close observer of human behavior. Yet man is more or less adept at reasoning, whether scientific, or mathematical, or philosophical; man is capable of technical invention and artistic creation; man can plan and predict; and all this is surely enough to justify our calling ourselves "rational."

It has often been suggested that this unlikely combination of mind and flesh is the root of man's deepest problems. Angels and beasts, we may be told, make some kind of sense, but a rational animal is a monstrosity. Whether there is any truth in this diagnosis of man's condition remains to be seen. What is certain is that man is a problematical creature. Animal though he is, he searches and probes and questions beyond every other animal's range of interest. Born into a vast material universe, he keeps wondering about what may lie beyond the material world. The

17

history of his speculations shows that just about anything within man's immediate experience can stimulate a line of questioning that drives straight to the ultimate issues of the origin and purpose of creation. It is true that when man seeks answers to ultimate questions he finds satisfaction with great difficulty, if at all. The answers that he learns or devises may not convince him. Earthbound philosophers may persuade him that there are no accessible answers about ultimate reality, or even that there is no reality beyond our world for us to ask questions and discover answers about. But the old questions keep recurring, sometimes in naïve, sometimes in subtle, forms, and it is at least arguable that nothing less than intellectual paralysis or anesthesia can keep man from pressing them home.

The great crises of human life seem to be especially important stimuli for ultimate questions. Great joys and great sorrows stir up man's heart and mind and make him unusually sensitive to the ultimate problems of human life and destiny. But of course no human experience forces such problems on us with the same urgency as the supreme crisis of death. "Throughout man's history," writes the psychologist Herman Feifel, "the idea of death has posed the eternal mystery which is the core of our religious and philosophical systems of thought." The same observation is reported more poetically by Charles Péguy:

> There is a residue of mystery in death, a centre, an abyss, a revelation of mystery—and quite independent of whose death, be it your father or your mother—every man is gripped. . . . The deafest hear, and the blindest see, and the closed are opened and even those who are armoured in insensibility bow their heads for a moment at a funeral.

No doubt men differ in the tone of their emotional response to the fact of death. Some may brood and shudder and tremble. Others may wrap themselves in careful forgetfulness or studied indifference. Still others may adopt a posture of heroic defiance. But no rational being, faced with inevitable death, can altogether close his mind to the nagging question of where he, a man, comes from and whither he is going. Is there more to human life than meets the eye of flesh? Has man a more than transitory place in the scheme of things? Is there really a scheme of things, an en-compassing order of reality, at all? The dark and challenging mystery of our human dying insistently poses these and similar questions and will not let us alone.

We must be sure that we understand the character of these ultimate questions. The question incessantly raised by the ex-perience of death is not simply whether life goes on. The obvious answer to that question is that the kind of life we know does not go on. Man really does die; his familiar existence under the sun, in the world of earth and wind and water, does come to an end. The real and serious question is something else again. Does man's earthly life enter into a larger pattern in which he occupies a permanent place as a conscious individual? Does his personal existence have a significance beyond the world of time and space? Has his life some value beyond his personal experiences and his activities in the world of creatures? To put it rather cryptically, does human personality have an absolute meaning?

But why, someone might well ask, do we need to take these questions seriously and try to find answers for them? Surely they are not so much rational inquiries as desperate outcries of a fevered imagination horrified by the thought of extinction. In sober reality there is no reason to make such a metaphysical fuss about dying. "The significant point is that, biologically speaking, natural death is not in the least mysterious, but is as understand-able as birth itself," writes Corliss Lamont. Why not take this final human fact as calmly as any other fact in our world?

The answer is suggested by the qualification, "biologically speaking." It is true that there is nothing particularly mysterious about the termination of a biological process. The cycle of animal life—birth, growth, maturity, senescence, death—is simply part of the order of nature, and no one finds it surprising or puzzling. But a human life is more than a turn of the wheel of nature. Every man is someone's child, and he may become someone else's parent, but he is more than a biological link in the long chain of the generations. Man thinks and desires and chooses. He enriches his mind with hard-won truth and tries to lead a life according

to reason. In a word, he is a person, capable of an individual perfection and worthy of a respect to which no mere biological unit
could (or would) aspire. It would be more than strange if such
a being did not wonder at the apparent extinction of his personality and did not feel driven to raise the question of ultimate
meaning.

Here we are, then, with a question that will not let itself be
ignored. As responsible human beings, we cannot do less than
face it squarely and see what we can make of it. As Christian
believers, entrusted with the word of life once spoken to a dying
world by the Lord of life and death, we are bound to try to
bring the resources of our faith to bear on the ultimate crisis of
man's earthly life. First of all, though, we must define our problem still more precisely. What do we mean by the ultimate
"meaning" of life?

A good deal of confusion is introduced into the discussion by
loose and exaggerated talk about the meaninglessness of human
existence apart from a life beyond death. Some overeager ex-
ponents of Christian teaching both misrepresent their faith and
weaken their case by asserting or implying that human life has no
point or value in itself, but derives all its meaning from its eternal
goal. This too simple argument has been damagingly outlined
and criticized by Lamont in a challenging modern criticism of
the doctrine of a future life:

> The great immediacies of experience cannot be an end in themselves;
> they have value only as a means to something else. Happiness and good do
> not and cannot stand on their own feet; they must have a justification in
> eternity. Thus the defenders of immortality find themselves in the awk-
> ward position of stating that it is futile and meaningless that things of such
> immense value as human personalities and human goods should endure in
> their valuableness for so short a time.

The point is well taken. And yet, surely even the clumsiest apolo-
gists for Christianity do not really mean what they seem to say. Is
it not likely that there are meanings and meanings, and that some
careful distinctions need to be drawn?

What do we mean by "meaning"? The question is harder than

it sounds, and it is not surprising that people get confused when they tackle it. Even the question of the meaning of words is tricky enough, as modern philosophical discussions have made only too plain, yet there our attention is fixed on three points: a symbol, a thought, and a thing. It may seem like borrowing trouble to transfer such an elusive term to the infinite complexity of actual human existence and expect it to prove a useful tool of thought. Nonetheless, I think that the word "meaning," thus broadly used, does refer to a recognizable aspect of human life, and that this reference can be defined clearly enough for our needs. To speak of the "meaning" of life is roughly equivalent to speaking of the "worth" or "value" of life. If there is any significant difference, it lies in the fact that "meaning" may suggest a relation to a more or less comprehensive purpose, in whose light worth or value is judged.

What meaning, then, can I reasonably claim for my individual life? At the very least, I can say that it is marked by countless meaningful moments, "great immediacies of experience" that I recognize as valuable and worthwhile. The love and the companionship of family and friends; glimpses of truth that excite and engage the mind; moments of generosity, when I really and readily give something of myself to others, and in the giving learn that in me there is something of genuine worth to give; perceptions of beauty, in a sound, a color, a soaring spire, a landscape, a child, that are almost too bright to bear—surely to have experienced all this and more is to have known meaning in my life.

But what about purpose? What about the thread that should link all my meaningful moments in a meaningful order? It is tempting to reply that if all else fails, I can make my own meaning by setting up my own goal and making all my choices with reference to it. But, in all honesty, what is this reply but sheer self-deception? To put it plainly, I am not my own free and undetermined creator. Within the limits imposed by my total environment, I can choose and devise and plan, but I did not make myself, my body, my brain, my temperament, and I am constantly and frighteningly dependent on wind and weather and other men for the continuation of my physical existence. On this showing, can my self-chosen purpose be anything more than a childish game, played defiantly in the face of hard facts? Must I not look for meaning in the world around me—the world that gave me birth and still sustains my life?

If I do turn to the world around me, I shall quickly find order of a kind—indeed, more than one order. For one thing, all lives fit somehow into the biological order of nature. As living beings, perhaps as parents, possibly as farmers or fishermen or miners, we all play a larger or a smaller part in the ongoing life of our species on the surface of this planet. For another thing, according to our opportunities we can take our place in society, and touch others' lives both in the constant give-and-take of personal relationships and through the institutions and traditions that we help to shape. In these ways, at least, our individual lives and actions and experiences enter into the real order of the world we live in.

The sense of meaningfulness that this kind of participation in the world of fields and sky, of animals and men, can arouse is movingly expressed by Willa Cather in *Obscure Destinies*. She has told the story of "Neighbour Rosicky," a remarkable emigrant from Central Europe who, after many trials in great cities, found a happy and useful life with his family on the American prairie. As the story ends, the young doctor is passing Rosicky's grave.

For the first time it struck Doctor Ed that this was really a beautiful graveyard. He thought of city cemeteries; acres of shrubbery and heavy stone, so arranged and lonely and unlike anything in the living world. Cities of the dead, indeed; cities of the forgotten, of the "put away." But this was open and free, this little square of long grass which the wind for ever stirred. Nothing but the sky overhead, and the many-coloured fields running on until they met that sky. The horses worked here in summer; the neighbours passed on their way to town; and over yonder, in the cornfield, Rosicky's own cattle would be eating fodder as winter came on. Nothing could be more undeathlike than this place; nothing could be more right for a man who had helped to do the work of great cities and had always longed for the open country and had got to it at last. Rosicky's life seemed to him complete and beautiful.

In a way this is a strangely appealing picture, and anyone who has really experienced the life of the countryside, close to the earth, will almost certainly find in himself something that responds to it. And yet, when we begin to think hard about it, we soon see that the attitude it reflects does not fully answer the question of purposeful meaning. It can be argued, of course, that there is no further answer, that the pattern of nature and history provides all the meaning that there can ever be in human life. But men do stubbornly raise a further question, and both honesty and prudence demand that we should face it. Again and again there bursts out in man a passion for the absolute, the infinite, the eternal, and that passion drives him to seek an absolute meaning for his existence. He may begin by asking simply whether the cycle of nature and the creative effort of human history fully explain and justify themselves, or whether on the contrary they derive their complete meaning from the plan of an all-seeing wisdom and the purpose of an all-ordering will. But eventually, somehow sensing within himself a mysterious kinship with that wisdom and will, he finds himself wondering whether the individual life—his own life—has a unique and abiding meaning in the all-embracing order of things. Rising above the incessant turmoil of finite things, his mind can form an idea of the eternal God. Will it ever find fulfillment in direct and absorbing communion with that God? Moving steadily and purposefully through the maze of choices and decisions that the world of creatures forces on him, his will can take on the shape of the Creator's will. Is there some transcendent purpose in this formation of moral character, this spiritual process that may go on even when physical life is withering away? Is a creature of eternal worth to be born of the travail of time?

It is questions such as these that the crisis of death poses with unique force. Is death the end not simply of a stage of human existence but of human personality as such? Does the fact of death mean that there is no point in expecting an ultimate fulfillment for each personal existence? Man has shown himself to be a seeker of meaning; is death the crushing denial of all hope of a goal beyond time—and therefore man's enemy? Or is there a further, fuller meaning for human life, of which death itself can be the instrument? Can we see in death not a literal "dead end" but the gate of life? All these questions cry out for an answer, if only we can find one.

By this time it should be clear that the desire for life beyond death springs from something deeper than a mere longing for permanence and a contempt for the transitory. The real question is not whether man's life goes on and on, but whether it goes to God. Does each moment of man's earthly existence simply point to another moment, and his whole life merely fit into the natural cycle of birth and death, birth and death? Or does his life, and each and every moment of it, point upward to a divine destiny—a completion in God and for God? No doubt such a destiny presupposes some kind of continuation of man's existence. But the point is that he should find fulfillment in God, not just that he should somehow survive, without rhyme or reason.

It should also be clear that the desire for life beyond death is something better than a naked hunger for the reward of virtue. The Christian idea of eternal life is often criticized by the high-minded unbeliever, on the ground that "it is more virtuous to act ethically without hope of reward than with such hope." This kind of criticism both misses the point of the Christian hope and suggests a rather aimless notion of ethical action. The real question is not whether man's good deeds are suitably rewarded in heaven, but whether all his actions can really be directed toward a transcendent goal. Let us tentatively define an ethical action as a responsible act rightly and duly directed to a reasonable end. On this showing, the ultimate ethical problem will be the identification of the authentic ends or purposes of human life. We must ask, for example, whether the moral quality of a human action is simply determined by its contribution to the survival of mankind as a biological species or to the efficient functioning of the human community. May it not be that the supreme consideration is the perfection of human persons as children of God, created in his image to find their completion in fellowship with him? No doubt such a fulfillment, presupposing as it does man's moral action, can be described as a reward of virtuous action. But the point is that man's actions should be intelligibly related to the divine purpose for human beings, not that they should be done for the sake of an external reward.

Perhaps our investigation of the problem of meaning in human life may seem to have become rather abstract, but the points that we have been considering can be illustrated quite concretely. I should like to discuss three typical human actions: the playing of a game, the creation of a work of art, and the performance of a work of mercy.

Let us suppose that I am playing a game with Anne, aged ten, and Sheila, aged nine, as I sometimes do. The atmosphere is warm and full of laughter, because we like each other and we think the game is fun. If I could spare a moment from trying to figure out the next move of my young friends, I might conceivably ask myself what this experience of playing together "meant." The immediately obvious answer would be that fun and fellowship among friends are a good thing—that this particular way of spending a little time is worthwhile and rewarding. In the present case this answer is so obvious that surely no one but a professor, and a ridiculously moralistic professor at that, would ever think of pressing the question any further. And yet, there is quite a lot more to be said, because no human action can be wholly isolated from whatever else the doer does or from what he is. Well then, what further meaning can I look for in our little game?

For me, at least, it provides needed and pleasant relaxation. (I doubt that the same could be said of my companions, whose approach to the game is not what one would normally call relaxed.) For us all it is a shared pleasure which, in spite of the occasional disagreement, draws the bonds of affection a little tighter. Undoubtedly it sharpens our wits, and it may even teach us emotional self-control. In old-fashioned language, it is an "improving" as well as an enjoyable experience.

Is there anything more to be said? Would it make any sense to speak of a simple game as having ultimate meaning? It would not, if ultimate meaning and permanence were one and the same. We do not want to go on playing our game for the rest of our natural lives, and I doubt that it figures in our picture of the joys of heaven. Nor do we expect its emotional effects to go on forever. I feel refreshed now, but before long I shall be tired again. We have been drawn closer together just now, but all too soon changing circumstances and fresh interests must begin to separate us. Then what remains? Just this: three children of God, who in a moment of happy companionship have learned a little more about meeting other people with honesty and forbearance—three children of God, who have opened their hearts to joy and, whether they know it or not, have thus become just a little more receptive to that supreme and eternal joy which is God himself. Surely that is meaning enough for a few minutes of play.

Again, let us suppose that I am writing a book—which is, in fact, what I am trying to do. Perhaps it seems a bit pretentious to call this effort the creation of a work of art, but I am doing my best to produce something that could decently be called literary, and literature is an art. I have been working on this project for a long time now, and it will not hurt me to slow down and ask myself what I really think I am doing. What does it "mean" to write a book?

I must frankly admit, to start with, that literary composition is not an unmixed pleasure. Collecting one's thoughts, groping for words, writing and rewriting, typing and retyping—the process is seldom easy, and sometimes each step is a painful effort. And yet, there is a delight that surprises me now and then as I work away, when a thought takes clean-cut shape in my mind and clothes itself in flowing words and almost puts itself on paper. Such delight, I suppose, is the first meaning of writing a book. But there is obviously more to it than that.

I shall not dwell on the external reward, in the form of royalty checks from the book publisher. If the author is lucky, his earnings may be substantial, and he will certainly accept whatever is coming to him without bashfulness, but he does not ordinarily set out to write a book as the quickest and easiest way of making a fortune. What drives him to write, and perhaps even to seek his livelihood in writing, is the persuasion that he has something to say and that he can find in himself the skill to say it.

Eventually, we hope, he gets his book finished—with what result? Inevitably, he will have learned something himself. His prolonged wrestling with ideas and words will leave him with an enriched mind; his disciplined application to a task will have hardened his moral muscle. Almost certainly, his book will find readers, and there is a fair chance that it will speak so directly to some reader's condition of mind and heart that his life will never be quite the same again. Mind will have met mind across the barriers of space and time.

When the labor of reflection and composition has borne such fruit, what more is there to ask for? If we raise the question of ultimate meaning, can we expect an answer? Once again, we must not confuse ultimate meaning with permanence. No writer wants to go on writing forever; no writer expects his books to endure forever. But a writer may well hope that what he has written will produce a transcendent effect. His book, after all, is addressed to human beings, and human beings—if the high doctrine of man's destiny turns out to be true—are called to eternal life in God. Perhaps our author has written about man or man's world. Then, if he has written well and truly, he has helped men to live their earthly life more wisely, more rationally, more sensitively, more nobly. Or perhaps he has written about God and God's love and grace. Then, if he has written faithfully and devoutly, he has helped men to see the goal of their earthly life and to find their way toward it. In short, in the one case he has helped men to become more genuinely human, and in the other he has pointed out to them the destiny in which their humanity will be fulfilled. What more could a man ask, than that his labor should thus serve the ultimate purpose of man's creation?

Finally, let us suppose that I have gone to pay a friendly visit to a sick person. The patient is an old friend of my family and my own lifelong friend. I sit down beside her bed, and we talk quietly about past days. We laugh together about the games we used to play with toy boats in the brook, when I was six and she was already past sixty, but still ready for mischief with a little boy. Her mind goes back to the time when she married and came to live near my grandparents in Nova Scotia, then to her own childhood on the islands of the Gulf of St. Lawrence. In vivid detail she describes her Confirmation in a little seaside church when she was ten years old. After an hour or so I get up to leave. My old friend thanks me for coming to see her, and we say good night. Technically, I have performed a "work of mercy"—visiting the sick. In fact, I have enjoyed an interesting conversation, shadowed only by the thought that there cannot be many more to come. What should I say if I were asked what the visit "meant"?

Once more, I could begin by pointing to a simple experience. Two friends met and enjoyed their meeting. For my old friend it was something of an event in what has become a very uneventful life; for me it was an interlude of quiet in a day full of activity; for us both it was a welcome revival of cherished memories. Whatever else there may have been to the visit, it meant these things at least.

I had set out to do a good turn, I intended to be kind to someone who had always been kindness itself to me. As so often happens, I found that in going to give I got more than I gave. My talk with my old friend was full of interest. So much the better! A little enjoyment does not take away the moral value of an action. Only a perverse rigorism can seriously maintain that no genuinely moral act is pleasant. I honestly meant to repay a moral obligation, and in my small way I think I did just that. In other words, my visit was not just a refreshing experience, because in making it I did perform a moral duty.

This very elementary moral action was a transaction between two human beings. I had received much from my friend, and I wanted to give something back. But is that all that can be said about it? What about the ultimate meaning of my action? Does it make sense to suggest that my simple gesture of friendship has some transcendent significance?

It does not, if what I am looking for is an external reward for a virtuous action—if I suppose that once I ascribe ultimate meaning to a moral act I can begin to write out a bill for submission in heaven. But it does make sense, if I think of the meaning of even the simplest act for my growth as a child of God. When I do a small act of kindness to another person, I am really expressing toward that person the love which I continually receive from God, and by thus imitating him in love I come—perhaps almost imperceptibly—closer to him. It is in such a drawing nearer to God that the ultimate meaning and the real reward of our good deeds will be found. If we could only remember that our moral actions have this depth of meaning, how seriously and responsibly our moral decisions would be made!

In these very personal illustrations I have been postulating a certain kind of meaning for human actions. Recognizing fully that transitory human experiences have their own intrinsic value, I have suggested that they may also have transcendent worth, insofar as they help to shape human persons for their final destiny in direct, unhindered communion with the Creator of all things. I have tried in some detail to show how certain simple but typical human activities would look in this perspective, and by now it may be fairly clear that such a vision of man's destiny ennobles human life and expands its meaning. But the decisive question has still to be faced: Is the vision truth, or is it illusion? We can scarcely postpone our answer much longer.

That means that the challenge of death must soon be squarely met. In the last few pages it must have been increasingly obvious, paragraph by paragraph, that our mortality sets the largest of all question marks over against the doctrine of man's transcendent destiny. It may be true that in the eyes of Christian believers the problem of sin looms as large as the problem of death, because to know our destiny in God is of no account if we deliberately reject it and cut ourselves off from it by sin. But the more ultimate question is whether we have a transcendent destiny at all, and we can deal with that question only by trying to unlock the secret of death.

II

Is death a blank wall, or is it a gate? The human mind quails at the mere thought of tackling a question of this size. Yet wise heads through the centuries have been convinced that no human question more urgently demands an answer, and in every generation brave souls have undertaken to provide one. Obviously, we shall have to take the plunge ourselves.

Once we have made up our minds to face the problem of death, it seems natural to look to our reason for a solution. After all, we are dealing with a universal human problem, to which some of the ablest, clearest minds in human history have given serious and prolonged attention. Surely a clear and cogent answer is not too much to expect from such a galaxy of brilliant and ardent lovers of wisdom.

Perhaps it should not be, but it apparently is. A clear and cogent answer is just what philosophy has not given us. Compared with their great rational discussion of the reality of God, the philosophers' reflections on human destiny seem thin and inconclusive. Moreover, when they do speak fully and definitely, what they have to say commonly proves strangely unsatisfactory—not just because we may find it disappointing, but because it leaves us with the feeling that approximately half the relevant evidence has been passed over lightly for the sake of a tidy solution. Somehow that awkward creature, the rational animal, consistently defeats the attempts of his own reason to understand his destiny.

For some of our most articulate philosophers the almost self-evident answer to the question of life and meaning beyond death is "No." Man is an animal, closely akin to other animals; he is born like an animal, and there is no reason to suppose that he does not die like one. As George Santayana expressed it in *Reason in Religion:* "The fact of having been born is a bad augury for immortality." If we try to console ourselves with hopeful speculations about man's spiritual soul, we shall quickly have the book of science thrown at us. In the past (we shall be reminded) many eminent thinkers have surmised that man's mental functions are completely dependent on his physical organism, and modern physiology and neurology have confirmed this opinion beyond any doubt. If we question the further step to the total rejection of the idea of the soul, we shall likely be told that this idea is a metaphysical notion—a final and crushing retort in the minds of those who use it. Man's destiny is purely and simply this-worldly, and bodily death means personal extinction. No transcendent expectation can be anything but illusory.

This philosophical judgment is definite enough, but for all its definiteness it has failed to carry everyone with it. There remain philosophers who are ready to defend the reality of the soul as the enduring spiritual core of personality, even at the cost of being called "metaphysicians." If men keep relapsing into metaphysics, despite the most intensive scientific therapy, these philosophers think they know why. There is in reality, they claim, something that is more than physical, and there is in man a peculiar capacity to respond to that something. Man's intelligence may necessarily rely on his nervous system to gather and file the data of thought, but reason itself and rational will are rooted in the spiritual soul and reach out beyond matter to God who is spirit. As spiritual personality, man is made for communion with the divine, and bodily death, far from being the end of his existence, is simply the gate through which he passes to his true destiny.

Those who maintain this conviction with all the self-confidence of the lawful heirs of a great tradition are not noticeably disturbed by the observation that the arguments in its favor are less tangible and down-to-earth than the evidence alleged by the opposition. They quite properly decline to surrender to the "scientism" for which the methods of the natural sciences are the only path to truth, so that any evidence which cannot be handled by those methods is not real evidence. But in acknowledging the strength of their position we must not blind ourselves to its serious weaknesses as a solution of the problem of death and ultimate meaning. For one thing, their zeal in the defense of spiritual reality too easily leads to an exaggerated "spiritualism." The distinction between soul and body becomes dualistic in tone. The soul comes to be thought of as the real man; both its independence of the body and its conflicts with the body are overstated; and death is presented as the soul's return from exile in the world of bodies to the true home of pure spirits. In this perspective, it is next to impossible to see any meaningful connection between man's earthly life and his eternal destiny. The quest for God becomes a movement away from the body, and man's experience in and through the body has no positive relation to the ultimate meaning of human personality. Furthermore, man's life beyond death really remains a great question mark. Even if we are convinced by the rational arguments advanced for the spiritual reality and immortality of the soul, we still have no idea what the soul does with its immortality. Certainly it is far from self-evident that separation from the body is one side of the coin and assumption into union with the divine the other side. In other words, we still need to be shown that death is the gate to life's ultimate meaning, and the history of thought suggests that we shall wait a long time for a cogent demonstration from the philosophers. (Even Plato, we may recall, fell back on poetic fantasy when he had to handle the question of human destiny.) Under the circumstances, we may well conclude that philosophical doctrines of human immortality are pretty cold comfort. "Death as the end of the arc of existence may be dreadful to contemplate, but an infinitely more appalling prospect is the eternal dying of an immortality without God." In other words, if immortality without ultimate meaning were the only alternative to sheer mortality, one would be sorely tempted to hope hard for extinction.

One line of thought does justice to man as an animal; the other line of thought does almost more than justice to man as rational; but where shall we find a doctrine that makes sense of man's life and destiny as a rational animal? Where but in the Christian faith, whose world view begins with God's creation of heaven and earth and ends with the resurrection of the dead and the life of the world to come. The Christian faith sees man as at once the child of the dust and the bearer of God's image, and it proclaims God's power to raise him from dust to glory. The Christian mind is aware that man is more than animal, yet it refuses to exclude the animal from God's purpose for man. From the New Testament onward Christian teachers have often made much of the duality of soul and body in man, but they have also insisted on the union of both elements alike in man's present existence and in his final destiny. Again, the Christian mind is aware that the quest for ultimate meaning is natural to man, yet it refuses to see the end of that quest as anything but God's gift of love. From a very early date in Christian history it has been the habit of Christian thinkers to take philosophical ideas of immortality into their theologies, but the secure foundation of their Christian hope has remained the Gospel, not of what man is by nature, but of what God has made him by grace. Christianity does not promise escape from half of what it means to be human; it proclaims the full salvation of human nature. Christianity does not suggest that death is anything but grimly real; it proclaims the resurrection of the dead. To Christian faith, death is neither a blank wall nor a gate that swings open at man's touch; it is the gate of eternal life, but only because it has been broken open by God's mighty arm in the death and resurrection of Jesus Christ.

On Easter Day, April 12, 627, King Edwin of Northumbria received Christian Baptism at the hands of Paulinus of York. In his *Church History of the English Nation,* the Venerable Bede reports the proceedings of the council at which the king and his advisers decided to seek Baptism. In the setting of our present discussion, a speech made by one of the chieftains is of particular interest. He said:

Your Majesty, when we compare man's present life with the time about which we know nothing, it seems to me to resemble the swift flight of a solitary sparrow through the banquet-hall where you sit dining with your thanes and councillors during the winter months. Inside there is a comforting fire that warms the room, while outside winter snowstorms and rainstorms are raging. This sparrow flies in quickly through one door of the hall, and then flies out through another. While he is inside, he is safe from the winter storms, but after a few comfortable moments he disappears into the darkness from which he has come. In the same way, man appears for a little while on earth, but of what went before this life and of what is to follow we know nothing. Therefore, if this new teaching has some more certain knowledge to reveal, it seems only right for us to follow it.

Under God's guidance, Bede goes on, the rest of the council gave similar advice, and the matter was soon settled.

Bede wrote his history about a century after Edwin's Baptism, and it is unlikely that he has given us a verbatim report of the chieftain's speech. Nevertheless, that speech as he presents it vividly expresses what has unquestionably been one of the strongest human factors in the spread of Christianity. The Christian faith supplies a definite and comprehensive answer to the question of human destiny. The Christian answer does justice to the whole of human life; it frankly accepts the tragic reality of human death; it proclaims the ultimate triumph of life over death by the power of God, the Creator of life. It is hardly surprising that such an answer should have won the allegiance of so many minds and hearts.

"There can be no question that Christianity came into being first and foremost as a death-conquering religion." But there can be no question either that the passing years have muffled the ringing tones of its death-conquering message. It is quite evident that a good many modern Christians—to say nothing of the world around the Church—have their doubts. The conviction of life beyond death is undeniably one of the points at which what Walter Lippmann has called the "acids of modernity" have eaten most deeply into the substance of Christian faith. Not long ago *The United Church Observer* (the official publication of Canada's largest Protestant church) asked its readers to rank a number of suggested sermon topics according to their personal preference. The results of this inquiry were very interesting. The topic in greatest demand proved to be "ways to increase religious faith." A substantial number of readers showed strong interest in various psychological and social effects of religious belief. "Immortality" and "death, judgment, heaven, and hell" were left at the bottom of the list. *The United Church Observer* sensibly warns us against hasty conclusions, but one fact is beyond dispute. A significant cross section of the Christian community—there is no reason to suppose that the United Church of Canada is unique in this regard—does not really want to hear the message which in other ages has irresistibly drawn men to the faith. Nor is there much room for doubt about the explanation of this fact. It can scarcely be suggested that the question of immortality seems irrelevant to human life in an age when the threat of sudden death hangs over whole cities and nations. The only plausible conclusion is that many modern Christians have grown so weak in their assurance of eternal life in Christ that they prefer not to have the question raised at all—either because they hesitate to face it without firm Christian conviction or because they suspect that their difficulties on this point are symptomatic of a deeper and total crisis of faith. The very issue on which the Church once spoke with such effective authority now proves too disturbing to contemplate, and the Christian preacher is asked to attend almost exclusively to the immediate problems of individual and social life.

It would be wrong to dismiss these modern Christians, with all their difficulties and hesitations, as insincere or faithless. Very often they show a stronger sense of Christian responsibility toward the world around them and a deeper concern for intellectual truthfulness than their more confident brothers. If they seem to bow too low before fleeting fashions of thought, at least they must be given credit for trying to keep faith and reason on speaking terms.

But sympathy for individuals must not be allowed to obscure the fundamental issue. An interpretation of human life which ignores the ultimate Christian hope may still retain certain genuinely Christian elements, but it has turned its back on the distinctive message of Christianity. The very core of the Christian Gospel is the announcement that through Jesus Christ God has overcome death and opened to mankind the gate of eternal life. In the long run, then, there can be no compromise between the supernatural Gospel of the transcendent love and power of God and the doubts or negations of a skeptical naturalism. Christianity will cease to be Christianity as the New Testament teaches it and the Christian centuries have understood it if it fails to set forth the message of Christ's death and resurrection as God's own answer to the ultimate questions of human existence.

This book is written from the standpoint of historic Christianity and addressed to men who are facing death—that is to say, to Everyman. I am convinced that the problem of meaning beyond death is the crucial question of human existence, and I believe that Christian faith has the definitive answer—God's answer—to that question. I believe firmly that the story of Christ's death and resurrection, which is the foundation of the Christian hope of life through death, is true. In this book I want to show three things in particular: how God's solution of the human mystery of life and death lies at the heart of the Gospel; how the great observances of the Christian life are designed to set it forth; and how even such an apparently simple undertaking as the faithful and wholehearted keeping of Lent and Easter can help Christian believers to make God's answer their own victory, because it draws them into closer union with their crucified and risen Lord.

CHAPTER 2

THE DIVINE MYSTERY OF DEATH AND RESURRECTION

Christians, to the Paschal Victim
Offer your joyful praises!

The Lamb the sheep redeemed:
Christ, of sin wholly guiltless,
Reconciled us sinners to the Father.

Death and life met in conflict,
In a stupendous contest:
The Prince of Life, once dead, reigns undying.
        —Latin sequence, eleventh century

I

About twenty-five years after the founder of Christianity died on the cross, the first great Christian missionary wrote a long letter to a group of new Christians. Not long before, he had spent eighteen months in the lively Greek city of Corinth, building up a Christian community of considerable size. Now, as he lived and worked across the sea in Ephesus, he kept hearing of disputes and disorders in the church he had so recently established. Eventually messengers arrived from Corinth with a letter full of questions about faith and worship and the rules of Christian living in a pagan society. St. Paul rose spectacularly to the occasion with what we now know as the First Epistle to the Corinthians, into which he put some of his fullest and deepest expositions of Christian teaching. As we look back, it is hard for us to feel anything but grateful to the troublesome Corinthians, whose quarrels and questions drew from their apostolic father in God such various treasures as his eloquent hymn to Christian love (1 Cor. 13), his two instructive discussions of the Eucharist and its place in Christian worship (1 Cor. 10:14–22; 11:17–34), his account of the primitive Christian creed (1 Cor. 15:1–5), and his tremendous delineation of the hope that Christian faith inspires (1 Cor. 15:12–58).

At the moment we are most concerned with St. Paul's presentation of the faith on which the Christian hope is founded. His statement of the basic Christian message is clear and unequivocal.

> Now I want to remind you, brothers, of the form in which I presented to you the good news I brought, which you accepted and have stood by, and through which you are to be saved, if you hold on, unless your faith has been all for nothing. For I passed on to you, as of first importance, the account I had received, that Christ died for our sins, as the Scriptures foretold, that he was buried, that on the third day he was raised from the dead, as the Scriptures foretold, and that he was seen by Cephas, and then by the Twelve.   1 Cor. 15:1–5

The Corinthian Christians, who seem to have been querying the reality of the resurrection, are unhesitatingly told that their very existence as Christians rests on the twofold truth that Jesus died and that he was raised from death. Apart from this "good news," with all its consequences for their own destiny, their faith would be "all for nothing."

The New Testament as a whole supports St. Paul. For all the great teachers of the apostolic Church, the Gospel of Christ's death and resurrection is the heart of Christianity. The same conviction has shaped the Church's life through the centuries. Of course, it is evident that the historic Christian faith includes many other truths. Looking backward, for example, we can see how the Christian evaluation of the Gospel events presupposes the divine mission and the divine identity of the man who died on the cross, and so points to the ultimate mystery of faith, the Trinity in Unity. Christ's death and resurrection mean what they do because he is God's eternal Son, born into our world in our flesh. Again, this time looking forward, we discover that the Gospel events have issued in a fellowship, a worshiping and praying and preaching community, which boldly baptizes its initiates into the name of the same Trinity in Unity, Father, Son, and Holy Spirit. Christ's death and resurrection touch us through the words and actions of the Church, which is his "body." But the crucial Christian message, which makes both transcendent faith and historic fellowship a living force among men, is the good news of Christ's dying and rising again. It is in these events that man finds the assurance of his destiny in God; it is from these events that Church and sacraments derive their power to lead men to God.

> . . . if Christ was not raised, your faith is a delusion;
> you are still under the control of your sins. . . .
> But the truth is, Christ was raised from the dead,
> the first to be raised of those who have fallen asleep.
>
> 1 Cor. 15:17, 20

The death and resurrection of Jesus Christ are God's final word to man, God's effectual summons to the attainment of life's final meaning.

Death and resurrection—it is in these two words together that the climactic good news of Christianity is summed up. Yet I suspect that many Christians wonder how they can make good sense out of such a paradoxical message. Death is the tragic question, not the triumphant answer.

> Death and life met in conflict,
> In a stupendous contest:
> The Prince of Life, once dead, reigns undying.

This we can probably understand, at least if we take it to mean that death is simply the defeated enemy, trampled under foot by the Prince of Life. But if we are told that there is more to the Christian message than that—that "once dead" is as positive and significant a part of the Gospel as "reigns undying"—then we may well be puzzled. What is death but the negation of life, a destructive force to be fought and beaten?

Of course, it is true that in the eyes of Christian faith death is a conquered enemy. If we turn, for instance, to the great songs of faith, we shall quickly see how the hymns of the resurrection give jubilant expression to the confident awareness of unbounded triumph.

> Death's mightiest powers have done their worst,
> And Jesus hath his foes dispersed;
> Let shouts of praise and joy outburst:
>   Alleluia!

> He is risen, he is risen:
>   Tell it with a joyful voice;
> He has burst his three days' prison;
>   Let the whole wide earth rejoice.
> Death is conquered, man is free,
> Christ has won the victory.

In hundreds of verses like these, Christians through the ages have pointed to Christ's resurrection as the victorious answer to the question of death.

But the great tradition of Christian praise has more to say than this. It includes a notable strain in which death itself is celebrated as the instrument of victory. Perhaps the outstanding examples are the great hymns of Venantius Fortunatus, still used in Christian worship after nearly fourteen centuries.

> Sing, my tongue, the glorious battle,
>   Sing the last, the dread affray;
> O'er the Cross, the Victor's trophy,
>   Sound the loud triumphal lay:
> Tell how Christ, the world's Redeemer,
>   As a Victim won the day.

> Abroad the regal banners fly;
> Forth shines the Cross's mystery,
> Where he, the Life, our death endured
> And, by his death, our life procured.

As believers like Fortunatus see it, the apparent defeat in death is the real beginning of the victory. Christ's death is not a tragic mistake, belatedly corrected by the resurrection. Christ's death is itself and (so to speak) in its own right the beginning of the end of death's reign over mankind.

This positive interpretation of Christ's cross is far from being a mere flight of poetic fancy. It has obvious roots in the New Testament itself. "For to those who are on the way to destruction," says St. Paul, "the story of the cross is nonsense, but to us who are to be saved, it means all the power of God" (1 Cor. 1:18). In another letter he speaks of "our Lord Jesus, who was given up to death to make up for our offenses, and raised to life to make us upright" (Rom. 4:24–25). Other writers make the same point. "For Christ himself died once for all, for sin, an upright man for unrighteous men, to bring you to God, and was physically put to death, but he was made alive in the Spirit" (1 Pet. 3:18). ". . . we do see Jesus, who was 'made for a little while inferior to angels, crowned with glory and honor' because he suffered death, so that by the favor of God he might taste the bitterness of death on behalf of every human being" (Heb. 2:9). "Jesus answered, 'The time has come for the Son of Man to be glorified. I tell you, unless a grain of wheat falls on the ground and dies, it remains just one grain. But if it dies, it yields a great harvest'" (John 12:23–24). Unquestionably the written trust deeds of our faith support the claim that Christ's death is an integral part of his triumph.

The essential point is this: God has answered our question from inside. The Lord of life has defeated death by dying. We may still have any number of questions left to ask about the way in which Christ's dying defeats death, but the central truth is plain. God did not solve the problem of death by ignoring it, as though it were a phantom of the mist soon to disappear in the light of the rising sun. God solved the problem of death by entering into it and transforming death. The eternal Son of God, born in time of a human mother, made bone of our bone and flesh of our flesh, shared to the full the common lot of humanity. He lived his human life through to the bitter end—the final catastrophe of death. It was then, and only then, that his human life reached its destiny. It was then, and only then, that his human life was taken up by divine power and carried across the boundary between time and God's eternity. Death was not just passed over lightly. Death was wrestled with and transformed from within, until the very event which seemed to destroy all hope of ultimate meaning became the final step toward ultimate meaning. Through Christ's dying the blank wall of death was changed into the opened gate of life.

To explain how this transformation was brought about, the New Testament makes extensive use of the concept of sacrifice. Jesus himself used the language of sacrifice at his "last supper" with his disciples.

As they were eating, he took a loaf and blessed it, and he broke it in pieces and gave it to them saying, "Take this. It is my body." And he took the wine cup and gave thanks and gave it to them and they all drank from it. And he said to them, "This is my blood which ratifies the agreement, and is to be poured out for many people." Mark 14:22-24

The Epistle to the Hebrews takes up this twofold sacrificial theme, with explicit reference to its background in the Old Testament system of worship.

He is taking away the old to put the new in its place. And it is through his doing of God's will that we have been once for all purified from sin through the offering of the body of Jesus Christ in sacrifice. . . . Christ has offered for all time one sacrifice for sin, and has taken his seat at God's right hand, from that time waiting for his enemies to be made his footstool. For by that one sacrifice he has forever qualified those who are purified from sin to approach God. Heb. 10:9-15

For if sprinkling ceremonially defiled persons with the blood of bulls and goats and with the ashes of a heifer purifies them physically, how much more surely will the blood of the Christ, who with the eternal Spirit made himself an unblemished offering to God, purify our consciences from the old wrongdoing for the worship of the ever-living God? And this is why he is the negotiator of a new agreement, in order that as someone has died to deliver them from the offenses committed under the old agreement, those who have been offered it may receive the unending inheritance they have been promised. Heb. 9:13-14

Other New Testament writers work with the same ideas (though in less detail), while the early fathers and historic liturgies of the Church treat them as normative for the interpretation of Christ's death.

In order to understand every detail of the texts just quoted, we should have to make a careful study of the sacrificial usages of the Old Testament, from which the symbols they contain are derived. Fortunately, we can draw out the central theme without stopping to consider each detail. The essential idea of sacrifice is a surrender for transformation—a letting something go from the human realm that it may pass over into the divine realm. In the case of material offerings, such as the animal sacrifices of the Old Testament, what happens is that an object is decisively and finally removed from human ownership and ordinary use and handed over to divine possession and use. By such an act the offerer intends to acknowledge the divine lordship or win divine favor and aid or enjoy divine fellowship.

As the great prophets of Israel, followed by the New Testament, make plain, no act of material sacrifice is really sufficient for these purposes. The object offered, however valuable it may be, is religiously significant only as the token of an inward and personal submission that may in fact be withheld. The offerer himself, however sincere he may be, is still a sinful creature, unable to rise to that total and unblemished offering of his free will which is all that any creature can ever have to give to God. If the Old Testament sacrifices were the whole story, the gulf between man and God would necessarily remain unbridged.

But the whole point of the New Testament is that the Old Testament is only the first part of the story. The message of the New Testament is that the gulf has been effectively bridged. The true and pure sacrifice of an unmarred, untainted human life has been made by Jesus Christ on his cross, and God's acceptance of that sacrifice has been unmistakably shown forth in the resurrection of Jesus Christ from the dead. In other words, a human life has perfectly realized its meaning as a human life, at every moment and in every action, and God has accepted that whole and perfect life and raised it to the eternal destiny for which each and every one of its temporal deeds prepared it. The perfect sacrifice has been offered and accepted; the perfect life has been lived and fulfilled.

In order to complete the New Testament picture of sacrifice

we must make one more point. Christ's offered and accepted sacrifice was not an isolated event. Christ's offering was made on behalf of mankind, and through it every human life can be made acceptable to God. The destiny attained by Jesus Christ is open to every man whose life becomes intertwined with his. The crucified and risen Christ is the "Adam," the "life-giving Spirit" (1 Cor. 15:45), of a renewed human race—a race whose life in time is already touched by eternity because he is in eternity. One human life story, marked from start to finish by entire surrender to God, has become the effective point of contact between the whole human race and its Creator.

But why, we may still wonder, should all this involve the death of the new "Adam"? His human will was perfectly conformed to the divine will; why would such total obedience need to be sealed by death? If the supernatural view of Jesus' life is true— if his entire life is a holy offering of perfect love and obedience, intrinsically acceptable to God—why should he undergo suffering and a death of pain and shame? It is mysteriously said of one legendary figure of the Old Testament that "Enoch walked with God, and he was not: for God took him" (Gen. 5:24, ERV). Might we not expect that the passing over of the perfect life from time to eternity would be a mystery of glory—the complete opposite of a brutal affair of wood and nails and bruised and torn flesh? We are told that the Gospel is the story of the divine victory over death; surely the fullest triumph over death is not to die at all.

The wisdom and righteousness of God's dealings with mankind can never be wholly grasped by man's mind, but I think our question has an answer that we can at least begin to understand. It is stated with supreme simplicity in the familiar lines by Cecil F. Alexander:

> He died that we might be forgiven,
>   He died to make us good;
> That we might go at last to heaven,
>   Saved by his precious Blood.

There was no other good enough
To pay the price of sin;
He only could unlock the gate
Of heaven, and let us in.

It is sin that makes death what it is for man. We do not need to speculate rashly about how man might have passed into eternity from a sinless world in order to see how sin colors the physical fact of death. Sin cuts man off from his true destiny by breaking the link between man and the living God. As separation from God here and now, sin threatens and foreshadows eternal separation from God in death. By isolating human life from the Lord of life, sin shrouds human death in final hopelessness. It is clear that sin has to be overcome if death is to be defeated.

In God's purpose as displayed in Christ, man's way back to life is a strange reversal of the process I have just described. "Sin is the sting of death" (1 Cor. 15:56), the source of death's despotic power over man. But now one man's death has paid "the price of sin" and brought man back to life. The Prince of life has come freely and graciously into our world of sin and death to lay down his own sinless life in death at the hands of sinners. His perfect sacrifice is something more than even the fullest submission of his life to God's purpose for human lives. It is a sacrifice for sin, a free offering of total obedience in and for a sinful world. Jesus deliberately and willingly accepts the conditions of life in a sinful world and does not draw back even in the face of undeserved death. His death, thus freely borne in faithful witness to God's truth, is accepted by God as the full and perfect act of atonement for the sins of the whole world. From now on men and women, reconciled to God by Jesus' atoning death, can look with confidence to God for final victory over their own death. St. Paul says:

If, when we were God's enemies, we were reconciled to him through the death of his Son, it is far more certain that now that we are reconciled we shall be saved through sharing in his life!   Rom. 5:10

But reconciliation itself remains the foundation of our hope, so that we are quite right to hail Christ's cross as the first sign of God's triumph over death.

Just one more question remains to be considered, and then our outline of the Christian Gospel will be as complete as it can be. I have been trying to tell the good news of God's victory over death, but most of the time I seem to have been writing the story of the death and resurrection of a man. What does it mean to call this human story a divine victory? It is easy enough to think of the resurrection as an act of divine power, but is God so deeply involved in the whole story that we can speak of his struggle and his triumph?

The Christian answer, of course, is that he is involved in the whole story. Christians believe in the unique value of Christ's life and death and resurrection because they believe that Jesus Christ is the unique Son of God, eternally one with the Father in being and in will. By itself, the incarnation—the birth of God's Son in our flesh—is not the Gospel, but without the incarnation there could be no Gospel of death and resurrection. That Gospel is essentially the story of God's remaking of human life and death from within. The divine Lord recalls human life to its eternal destiny by entering into it and living and dying. The key to the plot is the infinite love that brings the Lord of life to a sinful and dying race, to atone for its sins by his death. The climax of the tale is the restoration of reconciled mankind to communion with God through his risen and glorious Son. From beginning to end it is a divine story—the story of God who "loved the world so much that he gave his only Son, so that no one who believes in him should be lost, but that they should all have eternal life" (John 3:16). Take the divine hero out of the story, and we will have no Gospel left, no atoning sacrifice, no final victory.

It is God who remakes human life. But it is human life that is remade, and it is remade from within. If the doctrine of the incarnation assures us that God has taken action on our behalf, it also insists that he has taken action in our flesh. If the divinity of Jesus Christ makes our salvation sure, his humanity makes it our salvation. These different statements are all ways of putting same truth: that in the Gospel events human nature was God's real instrument. It was our life that the Son of God lived, our death that the Son of God died. His atoning sacrifice arose out of the divine love, but it was carried out by human obedience and completed in a human death. His final victory was the work of divine power, but it was prepared for by that same human death and accomplished in the human nature that he took in his incarnation. It is certainly true that the Gospel is the story of God's mighty acts, but it is no less true that what God has done has been done in and through and for our manhood.

The point is just this: the victory is God's, but it is a victory won for us, God's meaningful answer to a real human question. It is a victorious answer because it is God's own answer; it is meaningful to us because he speaks it in the language of human flesh and blood.

II

We have been looking at the very heart of Christian faith—the good news that God has overcome death and the sin that enslaves us to death. We have seen how in the death and resurrection of Jesus Christ God has acted to transform our life and our death. The death that was once the brutal denial of all transcendent meaning for human life has become the gate to ultimate and eternal meaning.

At this stage of our reflections on life and death and resurrection, two questions quite naturally come to mind. What can we know of the destiny that has been opened to us? How can we prepare ourselves to approach it? The destiny of which the Gospel speaks is our own destiny; what does it mean for our own lives? The destiny of which the Gospel speaks was won for us by God through human obedience and a human death; what are we to do in our turn to make it our own? To find answers we must turn back again to God's final word to man, the Gospel of Christ's death and resurrection.

In reply to our question about our ultimate destiny the Christian Gospel, carefully considered, has two things to tell us. Our best course will be to look at each point in turn.

On the one hand, the Gospel gives a negative answer. Eternal life is unlike life in space and time. Jesus did not merely, in St. Paul's words, become "once for all dead to sin" (Rom. 6:10); when he died on the cross he parted finally from the joys and sorrows, the relationships and duties, of earthly existence. For all their insistence on its objective reality, the Gospels will not let us think of the resurrection of Jesus as the revival of a corpse, a picking up of the threads of ordinary life after a brief interruption. No doubt when St. John tells the story of the raising of Lazarus he means us to take it as a sign of the same life-giving power that raised Jesus from the dead, but he carefully underlines the difference nonetheless. The Jesus who calls Lazarus out of the tomb says to the bystanders, "Unbind him and let him move" (John 11:44)—in other words, let him go back to the world and its work. The Jesus who rises from the dead needs nobody to unbind him, and his words to the eager Mary Magdalene tell of a heavenly mystery:

> "You must not cling to me, for I have not yet gone up to my Father, but go to my brothers and say to them, 'I am going up to my Father and your Father, to my God and your God.' " John 20:17

As the New Testament presents it, Christ's resurrection is not a sensational return from the dead to ongoing natural life, however appealing the idea may seem to superficial defenders of Christian truth. On the contrary, for the New Testament writers the resurrection is an exaltation of manhood beyond the limitations of nature and the possibilities of history. This is not to say that the resurrection was not an event in time—that "nothing happened" on the first Easter Day. But it is to say that what did happen was the taking up of Jesus' manhood into an eternal and unimaginable destiny, not its return to the familiar concerns of everyday life.

On the other hand, while the Gospel warns us against crude and mundane notions of the risen life, it has something positive to say as well. Eternal life may be unlike our present existence in space and time, but still it is life—a human life, a human hope, a human destiny. The resurrection of Jesus is not a resuscitation of his corpse for continued earthly functioning, but it most certainly is the raising up of Jesus. God calls Jesus from time into eternity, but it is Jesus who is taken up. The Jesus who appears to his disciples is strange and mysterious, but they recognize him nonetheless as the Jesus who was crucified. He is transformed and glorified, but it is Jesus himself who is transformed, and if he appears as risen and glorious it is because God has really raised him up at a particular moment in human history.

What all this means for our own destiny is clear enough. A hope which is securely based on the death and resurrection of Jesus Christ is not a hope of going on more or less as we are or of being brought back to our present kind of life—a hope, that is, which would add no new depth of meaning to our earthly existence, but would merely guarantee its indefinite continuation. The genuine Christian hope is the meaningful hope of reaching the goal at which our present existence aims—the final fulfillment of our completed lives in communion with God. And yet it is still our own life that is fulfilled, the life of human beings, transformed indeed through death and resurrection, but not destroyed. Perfected human beings will see God and love him and adore him, and God will see his own beauty and goodness and glory mirrored in human minds and hearts.

Perhaps this account of our destiny in Christ seems too general and indefinite to give much help to human beings in the particular and definite decisions that they must constantly be making. Indefinite it necessarily is, because the good things that God has prepared for those who love him surpass man's earthly experience and understanding, and at best we can sketch them only in rough outline. But it is full enough to provide us with the basic principles of an answer to our second question: How can we prepare ourselves to approach our ultimate destiny?

On the one hand, the transcendent character of the Christian hope points to detachment from all created things as one essential attitude of the Christian life. I do not mean, of course, that created things are to be treated as worthless. However often they may be confused, genuine detachment and unfeeling contempt are not at all alike. The Christian not only feels the attraction of creatures but also, because he believes in God the Creator, knows their real worth. But he knows too that the Creator is infinitely greater than the creature, and this knowledge determines his scale of values. The fundamental rule of human life must be the fulfillment of the Creator's purpose. If man's true destiny is eternal life in God, as the Christian Gospel asserts, then all that man learns and does and creates and enjoys must somehow serve that destiny. I am not suggesting that God is exclusively interested in man's religious consciousness, or that Christians must devote themselves wholly to prayer and religious studies at the expense of worldly responsibilities and activities. But I am concerned to make God's absolute claim on our lives clear. Perhaps four closely connected points will illustrate what I am trying to say. First, the ultimate meaning of our earthly life is the shaping of human persons for eternal fellowship with God. Second, what enriches a man as a human person, made in God's image, is good for him, while what merely satisfies an animal impulse, to the detriment of his personal integrity, is bad for him. Third, the only adequate basis for genuine fellowship among human beings is their concern for one another as persons, created for a fully personal perfection. Fourth, a man must be ready to put aside every human satisfaction that hinders him in the pursuit of his divine calling. The attainment of his eternal destiny, willed for him by his Creator, is to be his paramount concern, and no creature or creaturely experience can be allowed to distract him.

Yet on the other hand, just because man the creature is really called to eternal life in God, his creaturely actions and experiences have an infinite significance. Everything that he does and everything that happens to him contributes to the making or the unmaking of a person whom God has created for eternity. It is frequently suggested by critics of Christianity that belief in life beyond death makes action here and now less urgent. To put it crudely, if people are unhappy or sick or downtrodden now it does not matter too much, because a glorious second chance is just around the corner. Christians may sometimes fall back on considerations such as this in order to ease an unquiet conscience, but all they really prove is how little they understand of the Christian hope. A right understanding of the Gospel of the resurrection can only bring a new depth to the Christian's sense of responsibility for his decisions and actions here and now. Both duties performed and duties neglected have eternal consequences. If we maintain our own integrity and fulfill our responsibilities to our neighbors, we come closer to what God wants to make of us. If we compromise our integrity or ignore our duties to others, we fall short of what God expects from us. In either case, we are helping to determine what we shall be in the life to come. Can any man really understand this and still take his earthly duties and decisions lightly?

Detachment and responsibility—taken together, these two words sum up the demand of our destiny on our present existence. But if the Gospel of eternal life were nothing more than a demand, we should be in a bad way. We could work doggedly at detachment and responsibility all our life long, and in the end fall short of our goal. Left to ourselves, crippled by sin and powerless against death, we could have no real hope of fulfilling the ultimate purpose of our lives.

But of course the Gospel of eternal life is much more than a demand for human effort. The Gospel of eternal life is the good news that in his death and resurrection Jesus Christ has won the decisive victory over sin and death, and it is only against that background that the demand for detachment and responsibility makes real sense. Man is not expected to solve the problem of death and destiny for himself; God has already solved it, and man's task is simply to assimilate God's answer. In other words, in the God-Man Jesus Christ human nature has won its way through sin and death to its true goal, and the Christian life is meant to be a life in Christ, a living into Christ's victory. If detachment and responsibility must mark our Christian life (as they certainly must), they are not expected to issue fully formed from the resources of our own nature. Christian detachment and Christian responsibility are the moral expression of Christ's life in us—part of the living out of our union with the crucified and risen Lord—and it is only as such that they can bring us one step nearer to our destiny. St. Paul writes:

I have been crucified with Christ, and it is no longer I that live, but Christ that lives in me. The life I am now living in the body I am living by faith in the Son of God who loved me and gave himself for me.

Gal. 2:20

The character of the Christian life could hardly be better portrayed. The Christian life is my own life; I live and think and speak and do and suffer and die. But my life grows toward its final meaning only because it is not just my own life. Jesus Christ, the "Adam" of the new, victorious humanity, has already passed through death to eternal life, and he unites my life to his so that, living and dying in him, I may share his triumph. Steadily and surely I make my way to eternal life, because in Christ eternal life already touches and draws me. I live with Christ; I shall die with Christ; I shall live eternally with Christ. That, and nothing less, is what it means to be a Christian, living by faith in the crucified and risen Lord.

CHAPTER 3

ANTICIPATION: THE RED SEA

> Come, ye faithful, raise the strain
>   Of triumphant gladness!
> God hath brought his Israel
>   Into joy from sadness;
> Loosed from Pharaoh's bitter yoke
>   Jacob's sons and daughters,
> Led them with unmoistened foot
>   Through the Red Sea waters.
> —St. John of Damascus

I

The place is a great church in the ancient center of Western Christendom, the city of Rome. The day is Easter Eve, fourteen or fifteen centuries ago. The time is late at night.

As we look around, we see that the church is crowded with people eager to celebrate the mystery of Christ's death and resurrection. In a group by themselves we notice the "chosen ones," the men and women and little children who are about to be baptized into Christ. Soon they will be led away to the baptistery, to go down naked into the water and come out of it clothed in the innocence of newborn Christians. Meanwhile, they are waiting to receive their final instruction from the readings which form so large a part of the Paschal vigil.

A little while ago the church was shrouded in a darkness so thick that we could almost feel it. Then fire was struck from flint, and the great candle, symbolizing the rising Light of the world, was set up before the people. Now all the lamps are blazing, and the building is flooded with light. The reader moves to his desk and begins to read from the first page of the Bible.

> In the beginning God created the heavens and the earth. And the earth was waste and void; and darkness was upon the face of the deep: and the Spirit of God was brooding upon the face of the waters. And God said, Let there be light: and there was light.   Gen. 1:1–3, ERV

As we look and listen, we can hardly miss the point altogether. Perhaps our biblical knowledge is limited, so that we do not recall St. Paul's tremendous sentence: "For God who said, 'Let light shine out of darkness,' has shone in my heart, to give me the light of the knowledge of God's glory, that is on the face of Christ" (2 Cor. 4:6). But the liturgical drama that we are witnessing teaches the lesson plainly enough. If (it says to us) you really want to understand the Gospel of Christ's death and resurrection, you must try to see how those events enter into the eternal purpose of the Creator of all things. The same uncreated Light shines in creation and in redemption. The plan of redemption springs from the creative wisdom that numbers the clouds and calls the stars by name. The work of redemption is accomplished by the creative power that has brought all things out of nothingness. You must (the liturgy tells us) see nature and grace together, as parts of one divine plan.

While we are thus musing, the Paschal vigil goes on. Lesson follows lesson, as the reader unfolds the great themes of the Old Testament. The scene changes from the world of nature to the arena of human history, and the Creator of nature is portrayed as the Lord of history. In particular, he is shown at work in the crucial events of the history of Israel, shaping for himself a people to serve his redemptive purpose. Let us listen to the reader again, as he tells the greatest story of them all.

> And Moses stretched out his hand over the sea; and the Lord caused the sea to go back by a strong east wind all the night, and made the sea dry land, and the waters were divided. And the children of Israel went into the midst of the sea upon the dry ground: and the waters were a wall unto them on their right hand, and on their left. And the Egyptians pursued, and went in after them into the midst of the sea, all Pharaoh's horses, his chariots, and his horsemen. . . . And Moses stretched forth his hand over the sea, and the sea returned to its strength when the morning appeared; and the Egyptians fled against it; and the Lord overthrew the

Egyptians in the midst of the sea. . . . Thus the Lord saved Israel that day out of the hand of the Egyptians; and Israel saw the Egyptians dead upon the sea-shore. And Israel saw the great work which the Lord did upon the Egyptians, and the people feared the Lord: and they believed in the Lord, and in his servant Moses.   Exod. 14:21 ff., ERV

At last the readings come to an end. The catechumens troop off to the font like harts panting after the water brooks, followed by the urgent prayers of the Church. Preparations begin for the climax of the vigil, the great Easter Eucharist. Soon the newly baptized will return to claim their place at it. Meanwhile, we have a few moments for reflection on a second new idea that the liturgy has set before us.

We have already seen how creation and redemption belong together in the one eternal purpose of God. Now it is time for us to think about the sequel to that first lesson. Put very briefly, it is this: God redeems his human creatures and their world in his own chosen way, by acting in and through human history. The distinctive feature of our human existence is that we have a history. When we have said that God created planet or platypus, there is nothing more to be said. It may be that the planet came into existence suddenly, through a cosmic explosion, while the platypus is the outcome of long ages of evolution on the surface of the planet. But the essential point is that however God may have brought them into being, once they are created they just go on being themselves, monotonously and unimaginatively, as long as they exist at all. A planet may be smashed to bits in some vast catastrophe, and an animal species may become extinct or evolve into something else, but a planet does not invent explosives and an animal species does not improve itself by creating cultures and building civilizations. Man, on the other hand, either furthers or undermines God's work of creation by his own acts in the realm of human decision and action and complex interaction that we call history. It is into this web of human historical action, in which man can either complete or destroy himself, that God comes redemptively to guide and prosper man's creative work and draw all mankind to himself.

It follows that the great events of the Christian Gospel are not to be thought of as isolated divine acts—sheer bolts from the supernatural blue. It is God alone who redeems mankind, but he does his redemptive work in history and he really does it historically, making human decisions and human influences his instruments. Through a great network of human events he slowly and patiently works out his purpose, until at last his eternal Son is born in time and crucified and raised from death, and in his death and resurrection our common manhood is taken up from the world of time and history into eternity. Nor are these events the end of God's work in history. Until the end of time he will carry forward his loving purpose, touching men with his grace, drawing them into the fellowship of his Church, and preparing them for their completion in Christ.

In reality, then, God is present in all history, battling the ignorance and willfulness of sinful humanity and striving to realize his own eternal purpose, which is the final meaning of the whole created order and the true meaning of history within that order. Consequently, the Gospel of Christ's death and resurrection must be seen and understood against the background of the purposeful and unceasing activity of the Lord of history from the beginning to the end of the human story. Only in this way can we grasp its significance in the purpose of the transcendent Creator who brought the world and man into being. It is this lesson that the liturgy has been trying to teach us, by giving us nothing less than a short course in universal history, theologically interpreted, as part of our immediate preparation for the Paschal celebration.

The "chosen ones" reappear, washed and anointed and touched by the bishop's hand in blessing, and the Eucharist commences. Bread and wine, the outward tokens of our creaturely homage, are set on the altar. The celebrant summons us to lift up our hearts in thanksgiving to the Lord of all things. He recalls what God has done in our creation and redemption and tells how our Redeemer Jesus Christ has established this holy rite of communion with himself in his sufferings and his glory. He prays that the gifts offered according to Christ's institution and hallowed by his word of power may be accepted by God as a true and worthy memorial of his Son's sacrifice, and that we who offer and receive them may be filled with heavenly blessing and grace. The holy bread is broken for distribution among us, and our Lord's own prayer is said. Then at last, enlightened by the truth of creation and redemption and mindful of Christ's death and resurrection, we go forward to take the bread of heaven and the cup of salvation, in full assurance of our place in the purpose for which the world and man were made.

II

My little essay in historical imagination has one purpose only. By and large it is authentic enough, but it is not meant to be an exact reconstruction of the past. It has been devised with the sole intention of illustrating the place in historic Christianity of one urgent conviction: that the Gospel of Christ's death and resurrection must be interpreted as part of the one divine plan by which the whole universe of creatures is ordered. The same Christian faith that sees God's hand in the death and resurrection of Jesus finds him at work, wisely and purposefully, throughout nature and history, and Christian believers are persuaded that all his actions, from the setting of the stars in their courses to the events of the Gospel, are directed to one all-embracing end.

In Christian eyes, the very heart of this all-encompassing purpose of God's creation is the total fulfillment of personal beings. That does not mean, of course, that the whole universe exists purely and simply for the support and instruction, let alone the entertainment, of rational creatures. By the mere fact of its existence the entire cosmos reflects God's being and goodness and so gives him glory. But it is in rational creatures alone that the universe comes alive in conscious response to God and freely serves his purpose. They are "priests" of creation, who take possession of its wonders by force of mind and heart and hand and offer them up to their Creator in spiritual worship, and in their destiny the whole world is exalted.

I have spoken of rational creatures, and not simply of human beings. Genuine Christian teaching does not involve the ridiculously presumptuous claim that in God's vast universe only human persons respond to him in love and worship. From the first, Christian theology has consistently recognized the immense range of God's creative power and purpose. For one thing, it has always been interested in the biblical allusions to "angels," and has commonly represented these beings as glorious spiritual creatures, conspicuously superior to man and called to no less splendid a destiny. More than once, too, theologians have speculated without a sign of nervousness about the existence of rational animals other than man, and modern Christian thinkers are facing with equanimity the possible discovery of intellectual life on other planets. Perhaps many skeptical minds will regard angels and Martians as equally dubious hypotheses, but that is not the point at issue. The significant fact is that the Christian mind has room for myriads of rational creatures, man's equals or man's superiors, and that it has no interest in rejecting whatever evidence there may be for their existence.

For Christian thought, then, man's destiny is typical of the destiny of personal beings in God's purpose, and Christian statements about man's fulfillment in union with God are not meant to be taken exclusively. According to Christian teaching, everything that exists was created by God through his eternal Word, and every rational creature, wherever he may be in God's universe, bears a profound and indelible resemblance to that same Word through whom he came into being. Consequently, the consistent Christian thinker cannot see how any rational creature can ever find full perfection and complete satisfaction short of the transcendent destiny that was disclosed when for us men and for our salvation the creative Word once took manhood, never to lay it off, and in that manhood died and rose from death. If human existence finds its ultimate meaning in eternal life, the same must surely be said of any other form of personal existence. How God achieves his purpose in other personal beings we may not know, but what that purpose is we can hardly doubt.

We can hardly doubt the incomparable wealth of God's loving kindness toward his rational creatures, for the very good reason that the dying and rising again of Jesus Christ have opened our eyes wide to our own destiny as God's children. In those tremendous events Christian faith sees disclosed the secret of the universe. To say this is not to ignore the fainter intimations of immortality that have cheered men's hearts and enlarged their vision of human life and its responsibilities. Again and again through the centuries human longings have fostered the hope of a destiny beyond death and human minds have sought and found reasons to sustain that hope. Among the people of the Old Testament, prophetic insight slowly but surely inspired the conviction that God's plan for human beings reaches beyond the grave, and the forms which that conviction took have influenced the details of Christian teaching itself. But only the actual triumph of our manhood over death in the cross and resurrection of Jesus Christ has directly and clearly revealed the mystery. Whatever tokens of the divine purpose may be found in the created world itself or in the earlier phases of God's self-revelation in human history, it is the Gospel alone that securely establishes the hope of eternal life.

The unique significance of the work of Christ has been repeatedly affirmed in the preceding chapters, and the claim cannot be made too emphatically or too often. But there is another side to the story, and that is what this chapter is mainly about. When we say that Christ's death and resurrection lead us into the very heart of God's all-embracing purpose, we take it for granted that God is real and that he really has a creative plan. We may claim that the Gospel is the spectacular final chapter in which all the threads of the long and varied story of God's works are drawn together, but in making that claim we are already assuming a divine author and an essentially coherent story. Apart from these presuppositions the Gospel itself would not be meaningful, nor even credible.

Perhaps this assertion seems extravagant, but let us test it by looking briefly at the story of Christ's resurrection from the dead. If the story is true, the sting of death has been drawn. But why should we think that it is true? There is no point in pretending that it is an easy story to accept. We are asked to believe something that has no parallel in our entire experience of life and death. The Church proclaims it as she has received it from her first teachers, Christ's apostles, and it is evident that they taught it with unwavering assurance. But it is tempting to think that their assurance was based on something that we can explain from our ordinary experience—on almost anything, in fact, except an actual resurrection. Resurrections, we tell ourselves, just do not happen. If the apostles believed, as they clearly did, that Christ had been raised from death, the explanation must be that intense hope produced hallucination, or that loving devotion simply could not accept the defeat of an adored master by death, or that the conviction of Christ's unique spiritual importance found expression in symbol and legend which a naïve age too readily took for historical fact—in short, nearly any explanation that stays inside human limits. The literature of modern biblical studies contains many ingenious examples of this sort of interpretation. Of course, it would be unfair to suggest that "liberal" scholars deliberately set out to explain away the core of the apostolic message. Their sincere concern is to get at the historical reality behind the strange and difficult and sometimes obscure statements of the New Testament. The only trouble is that they tend to assume that the historical reality for which they are searching must fit snugly into the framework of common human experience. This assumption has very serious consequences for their study because it obscures the essential character of the resurrection event as the New Testament writers understood it.

As the earliest Christians saw it, the resurrection of Jesus was not just a startling freak of nature. They knew as well as we do that in the workings of nature resurrections simply do not happen. "Because of their relation to Adam all men die" (1 Cor. 15:22), wrote St. Paul, going on to make it clear that nothing in our natural inheritance justifies the least hope that the process may reverse itself. The resurrection of Jesus is a supernatural event, a creative act of God himself. "God set aside the pain of death and raised him up, for death could not control him" (Acts 2:24). Only in these terms can the resurrection be believed and preached.

But the primitive Christian witness goes still further. As we have already noticed, the New Testament writers did not think of the resurrection as a "miracle," if by that we mean simply an unpredictable restoration of nature by the Creator of nature, when all natural forces have failed. As everyone knows, the Gospel narratives are full of strange stories of the renewal of natural functions—the return of the demented to sanity, the healing of bodily ailments, the giving of sight to the blind, even the raising of the dead—but the resurrection of Jesus does not belong among these events. It is not a miraculous return to natural physical life, but the beginning of a new life, the inauguration of a new age, the creation of a new world—an act of God which transmutes the natural human life of Jesus, the crucified, dead and buried Saviour, into a heavenly reality. St. Paul puts it in the right perspective when he tells his Corinthian converts about the nature of their own resurrection.

The body is sown in decay, it is raised free from decay. It is sown in humiliation, it is raised in splendor. It is sown in weakness, it is raised in strength. It is a physical body that is sown, it is a spiritual body that is raised. If there is a physical body, there is a spiritual body also. This is also what the Scripture says: "The first man Adam became a living creature." The last Adam has become a life-giving Spirit.   1 Cor. 15:43–45

Christ has really risen, but he has risen to a life beyond our earthly imagining.

In keeping with the character of the event they are affirming, the New Testament writers do not linger over the ambiguous fact that the tomb in which Jesus had been buried was found empty on "the third day." By itself that piece of evidence, however painstakingly verified, could never prove the claim the apostles are making, and in the New Testament presentation of the resurrection it plays a quite secondary role. The first Christians have a supernatural event to proclaim, and they support their preaching by an appeal to supernatural experience. Jesus, they insist, has really appeared in his risen glory both to his chosen apostles and to a wider circle of believers. Human eyes have seen the exalted Lord and in him have recognized Jesus of Nazareth who was crucified. It is on the strength of this direct evidence that the Church sets out to convert the world to the confession of Jesus as Lord.

The apostles testify to their supernatural experience of the glorified Christ and passionately urge us to accept their testimony. If we listen attentively, our hearts can scarcely help being touched by their message of eternal hope. But almost certainly our minds will be full of doubts. If the resurrection was incredible as a work of nature, has it become any more credible as a supernatural event, witnessed to by a handful of first-century Jews? Supernatural events do not sit comfortably on our twentieth-century minds, suspicious of any claim to knowledge beyond the reach of scientific exploration, and we wonder what there can possibly be in so strange a story, coming to us out of the dim past. How (we ask ourselves) could anyone really be expected to accept such astounding statements as true? What evidence could possibly be compelling enough to justify such a tremendous claim? How could the alleged witnesses make such assertions with such complete assurance? However great the confidence with which men testify to the incredible, must we not conclude that they are mistaken?

This is not the place for an argumentative defense of the traditional Christian view of the resurrection of Jesus. What I have in mind is much simpler. I want to suggest what it was in the mental outlook of the first Christians that made the announcement of the resurrection meaningful and credible to them. It was certainly not the complete absence of a tough-minded skepticism. The Gospel of John, for instance, paints a lifelike portrait of a very early doubter.

But Thomas, one of the Twelve, who was called the Twin, was not with them when Jesus came in. So the rest of the disciples said to him,

"We have seen the Master!"

But he said to them,

"Unless I see the marks of the nails in his hands, and put my finger into the marks of the nails, and put my hand into his side, I will never believe it!"   John 20:24–25

There will be no credulous acceptance of hearsay evidence for him. Yet of course "doubting Thomas" does finally surrender to faith, overwhelmed by the sight of the risen Lord, whereas it is easy enough to picture the modern skeptic, faced with the same evidence, repeating doggedly to himself, "There must be another explanation." We still have to find out what it is that makes the difference.

I think that the basic answer is quite simple. The difference is not so much between two historical epochs as between two contrasting habits of mind. The mental universe of the early Christians was wide open to the supernatural. By this I do not mean that as a body they were avid seekers after marvels and portents. In view of the popularity in every age (including our own) of astrology, spiritism, healing cults, and many other strange and wonderful enterprises, it is likely that a fair number of first-century Christians were superstitious. But Jesus himself had warned against reliance on signs and wonders, and the hostility of Christians toward the legends and superstitions of popular religion became so notorious that they found themselves denounced by their pagan neighbors as "atheists." The supernaturalism which distinguished the early Christians from most of their contemporaries (and from most of ours) was something quite different, then, from a preoccupation with the magical and occult. Briefly outlined, it consisted of a living faith in the sovereign reality and power of the transcendent God and a firm conviction that the world and man exist to fulfill God's purpose.

The New Testament repeatedly reflects the constant concern of early Christian teachers to fix this world view in the minds of their hearers. In Jewish circles, of course, where the Old Testament is accepted as the record of God's self-disclosure, a genuine supernaturalism can be taken for granted, and the apologetic task of the Christian preacher is simply to show how the story of divine revelation has reached its climax in Jesus the Messiah. Pagan listeners, on the other hand, have to be led step by step to the realization that "there is just one God, the Father, who is the source of all things, and for whom we live" (1 Cor. 8:6), and one of the most consistent features of early Christian teaching is the care that is taken to lay this foundation for the preaching of the Gospel.

Like the Jewish teachers who preceded them into the pagan world, early Christian missionaries were quite ready to exploit whatever leanings toward monotheism they could find in the philosophy of the day. St. Paul, we are told, went so far in a speech at Athens as to quote a Greek poet in support of the Christian doctrine of God the Creator (Acts 17:28). But as he soon found out, the mere notion of a single divine principle of all things was not enough to provide a firm basis for the Gospel of the resurrection. What was needed was knowledge of God as purposeful and active in nature and in history. In order to instruct their hearers in this truth, Christian teachers had to make full use of the Old Testament. Since early Christianity saw itself as fulfilling the expectations and thereby superseding the religious practice of Judaism, the appeal to the Old Testament was not without its awkward moments. But the Church fought fiercely against all attempts to dismiss the Hebrew scriptures as irrelevant to Christianity, because she saw clearly that the God of the Gospel was the God of Israel's history and Israel's faith and that the New Testament necessarily rested on the foundation of the Old.

The holy and eternal God has given being to a world, and in that world he has set man, created in his own divine image. God has been at work through all the vicissitudes of human history, striving to carry out his purpose for man and through man, despite the obstacles thrown up by human folly and human sin. In particular, he has called and formed for himself a people designed to be the instrument of his gracious will. The careless sinner and the anxious believer alike may more or less completely fail to see and understand the signs of God's patient handiwork. But his servants the prophets have learned to see his mercy and judgment in action in his people's history, working out his creative plan, and in the light of that vision they survey all history and the whole wide world with unshakable confidence in the power and love of the living God. This prophetic faith, and it alone, provides the supernatural soil in which the supernatural Gospel can take root and grow, and it is not surprising that the Church should so insistently introduce all who would understand and share her faith into the supernatural world of the Old Testament.

A few pages back, when I was describing the ancient Paschal vigil, I singled out two of its traditional readings: the sublime tale of creation and the story of the Exodus of Israel from Egypt. Perhaps we can now see more clearly than before why those two stories are so important for Christians. Between them, they spell out the essential preamble to the Gospel of Christ. God (they tell us) created man in his own image to find fulfillment in his perfect service, and the same God has chosen Israel to be the agent of his purpose for man. In the kind of world that these statements describe, Christians can confidently put forward their own distinctive claim, that God has decisively accomplished his purpose for mankind through Jesus of Nazareth, the true Messiah of Israel. Against the background of Israel's faith, even the most startling affirmations of Christian faith begin to make real sense. God has brought the world and man into being. In the turmoil of human history God has acted to work out his will for man. We cannot quite say that what comes next is "natural," because the destiny brought to light through the Gospel lies beyond the reach of human nature and out of sight of natural reason. But we can say that to those who really know the Old Testament, the Gospel of Christ's death and resurrection is not incongruous or altogether strange. God has shaped our manhood

in the likeness of his own eternal and glorious being. God has declared his concern for man by taking a mysterious part in the
drama of human history. This much we have grasped from the
Old Testament. If we are now told that God, by a supreme act
of mercy and might, has called that human nature which he has
created and cherished to eternal life, we may suspect that the
news is too good to be true, but we cannot deny that it fits together with the other steps of the story to form a meaningful
pattern. In a world artificially trimmed down to suit a narrow-
minded naturalism, there is no room for the supernatural. But in
the real world, created by divine power and ruled by divine purpose, while supernatural events may not be expected as a matter
of course, there is nothing inherently incredible about them. If
the Gospel of the crucified and risen Lord is clearly and strongly
attested by competent witnesses, we have good reason to receive
it as God's truth.

Of all the Old Testament stories that have contributed to the
full world view of Christian faith, it is perhaps the story of the
Exodus that has made the deepest impression on the Christian
imagination. It is not too hard to see why. No doubt the historians will tell us that the biblical account of Israel's formation
as a people and its entrance into Canaan is both oversimplified
and encrusted with legend, but that does not matter now. The
significant fact is that the story of the Exodus, as it took its
familiar shape in Hebrew tradition, became the great symbol of
God's care for Israel—a kind of shorthand sign for the complex
network of events through which Israel was called and consecrated to be God's holy nation. Seen in this light as the crucial
redemptive event in Old Testament history, the episode of the
Exodus inevitably attracted close and prolonged attention from
Christian believers, who looked to the Redeemer of Israel for
their own salvation.

The harder Christians looked at the story, the deeper their
interest grew. In their eyes the Exodus came to be much more
than one stage in God's preparation for the incarnation and
death and resurrection of his Son. They were so struck by a

strange parallelism between the event of the Exodus and the event of the Gospel that they began to see in the one a fore-shadowing and anticipation of the other. In the Exodus God rescued his people from bondage to the Egyptians; in Christ's death and resurrection he redeemed mankind from slavery to sin and death. Through the Exodus God led Israel to fulfill its historic destiny in the land of promise; through Christ's death and resurrection he led the human race to its final perfection in the land of eternal life. Even the details of the Exodus story seemed to prefigure the Christian Gospel. To win its way to safety, Israel passed through the midst of the sea, with the threatening waters heaped up on either side. To carry out the work of man's salvation, Christ passed through the dark waters of death. Read in this perspective, the Exodus story was already pregnant with the hope of eternal salvation, while the Gospel events appeared as the "new Exodus," fulfilling the promise of the old.

If we think that this linking together of the Exodus and the Gospel is nothing but an arbitrary juggling with symbols, we shall do well to think again. No doubt the symbolic or "typological" interpretation of Old Testament events can easily become strained and artificial. But the underlying idea is sound enough, and Christian thought has been enriched by its judicious applica-tion. From the beginning of creation to the end of time God's purpose is one and the law of his working is one. The same wisdom and the same will created the world and man, made the scattered tribes of Israel into an instrument of divine purpose, and won the final victory over sin and death. Is it altogether sur-prising that the works of one purpose should be so closely akin that one can serve as the living symbol of another?

Let us return in imagination to the place where this chapter began—an ancient church in the great city of Rome. By this time it is Easter night, and Christ's people are at their evening prayers.

As we come in they are just beginning to sing a psalm. Its haunting melody is thought to be one of the many heirlooms that

the Church has received from her Jewish parent. Let us listen
carefully to the singing.

When Israel came out of Egypt, and the house of Jacob from among the
strange people,

Judah was his sanctuary, and Israel his dominion.

The sea saw that, and fled; Jordan was driven back. . . .

Not unto us, O Lord, not unto us, but unto thy Name give the praise;
for thy loving mercy, and for thy truth's sake.

Wherefore shall the heathen say, Where is now their God?

As for our God, he is in heaven: he hath done whatsoever pleased him.

Their idols are silver and gold, even the work of men's hands. . . .

They that make them are like unto them; and so are all such as put
their trust in them.

But thou, house of Israel, trust thou in the Lord; he is their helper and
defender. . . .

The dead praise not thee, O Lord, neither all they that go down into
silence.

But we will praise the Lord, from this time forth for evermore.

Pss. 114–115

Perhaps we are tempted to ask just what the Church is prais-
ing God for. She seems to be singing about the Exodus, and yet
today is the feast of Christ's resurrection. Which does she really
have in mind?

The right answer is: Both. The Church does not try to separate them, because she knows that they belong together as fore-
shadowing and fulfillment in the one purpose of the Lord who
made heaven and earth.

PART TWO
SACRED SIGNS

CHAPTER 4

INITIATION: BAPTISM

> With Christ we share a mystic grave,
>   With Christ we buried lie;
> But 'tis not in the darksome cave
>   By mournful Calvary.
>
> The pure and bright baptismal flood
>   Entombs our nature's stain:
> New creatures from the cleansing wave
>   With Christ we rise again.
>   —John Mason Neale

I

One spring day, in or about A.D. 30, Jesus and his disciples were walking toward Jerusalem through the countryside east of the River Jordan. Jesus was resolutely setting the pace and the rest were following, full of foreboding. For some time now he had been trying to prepare them for the final crisis of his ministry. They still did not really understand what it was all about, but they knew enough to be thoroughly frightened.

As the little party came close to the old town of Jericho, Jesus made another attempt to show his followers what was coming. He took the inner circle of twelve apostles aside and predicted in brutal detail what would happen when they arrived in Jerusalem. The only recorded response was a piece of arrogance unmatched in the subsequent history of Christianity.

> And Zebedee's two sons, James and John, came up to him and said,
> "Master, we want you to do for us whatever we ask."
> He said to them,
> "What do you want me to do for you?"

71

> They said to him,
> "Let us sit one at your right hand and one at your left, in your triumph."
> Jesus said to them,
> "You do not know what you are asking for. Can you drink the cup that I am drinking, or undergo the baptism that I am undergoing?"
> They said to him,
> "Yes, we can."   Mark 10:35–39

The little dialogue would be nothing but a painful instance of human stupidity and conceit, if it were not for two things. The first is the fact that the episode drew from Jesus his great definition of the nature of Christian authority, culminating in the tremendous declaration: "For the Son of Man himself has not come to be waited on, but to wait on other people, and to give his life to free many others" (Mark 10:45). The second is the way in which Jesus shed light both on the meaning of the Gospel and on our relation to it by his challenging use of the symbol of "baptism" to represent his redemptive death. This second point is especially important for our study, and I want to develop it in this chapter.

Unless we are very careful, the deep meaning of this particular use of ritual language to describe the flesh-and-blood event of Jesus' death on the cross may escape us. We are used to hearing that death referred to as a sacrifice, and even if our knowledge of ancient sacrificial rituals is very sketchy, the phrase "the sacrifice of Christ" immediately suggests to us the picture of Jesus dying on the cross in the fullest self-surrender to his Father's will. But we do not readily think of "the baptism of Christ" as a parallel phrase. It has an obvious and literal reference to Jesus' ritual baptism at the commencement of his ministry, and we feel no compulsion to explore its meaning any further. If we come across one or two sayings in which Jesus speaks of his "baptism" as a future event, it is easy for us to find no more definite religious significance in them than we should see in a passing allusion to a regiment's "baptism of fire."

Yet Jesus himself clearly meant his references to his impending "baptism" to be taken very seriously. He used the word to convey to the sons of Zebedee the fearful implications of their request,

In a series of sayings on the critical urgency of his mission he had already spoken in similar terms. "I have come," he said, "to bring fire down to the earth, and how I wish it were kindled already! I have a baptism to undergo, and how distressed I am till it is over!" (Luke 12:49–50). In his eyes, his water baptism is quite evidently the sign of something greater. It is his consecration to his redemptive task, the first step on his way to the cross, a pledge that is to be fulfilled in the awful reality of his atoning death. If his death is the true and perfect sacrifice, it is also the true and perfect baptism.

The background of Jesus' language is unmistakable. Among the Jews of his day, ritual baptism already signified a transformation so complete that it could be spoken of as a death and a rebirth. The baptism given by John the Baptizer, to which Jesus so surprisingly submitted, was a "baptism of repentance," a sign of a radical change of mind and heart, a preparation for the new life of God's kingdom. The baptism administered to converts to Judaism, in order to purify them from the defilements of paganism, was a "baptism of regeneration," a sign of death to the old way of life and of birth into the holy community. Minds that were used to thinking in these terms would naturally understand what Jesus had to say about his "baptism" as a prediction of a transforming crisis.

A striking remark by St. Paul may shed a little more light on what Jesus had in mind. The apostle is emphasizing the unity of God's purpose throughout the biblical history. He writes:

. . . our forefathers were all protected by the cloud, and all passed safely through the sea, and in the cloud and the sea all, as it were, accepted baptism as followers of Moses, and all ate the same supernatural food and drank the same supernatural drink—for they used to drink from a supernatural rock which attended them, and the rock was really Christ. . . .

1 Cor. 10:1–4

Along with other things that we cannot stop to explore, St. Paul's words suggest that he had learned as a student of the Hebrew scriptures to think of the Exodus as a corporate baptism of Israel. It would not be strange, then, if Jesus himself had been acquainted with that idea. If we could only suppose, further, that he connected his death with the Exodus, we should be well on our way to a fuller understanding of his sayings about his "baptism."

The necessary link is hinted at by St. Luke in his account of the transfiguration of Jesus on the mountain in the presence of Peter, James, and John. Like the other evangelists, he tells how the two great Old Testament figures, Moses and Elijah—standing respectively for the law and the prophets—appeared in glory to talk with Jesus. But Luke adds a note on the subject of their conversation. They spoke, he says, of Jesus' "exodus" which he was going to carry out at Jerusalem (Luke 9:31; Greek text). There is at least a fair chance that St. Luke's language is more than merely accidental, and that he means to suggest the idea of Jesus' death and resurrection as a new Exodus. Is it too far-fetched to argue, putting these bits of evidence together, that Jesus himself may well have seen his impending death as a "baptism," just because he saw it as the first step in the new Exodus? From his early childhood he would have heard of the passage through the waters that freed God's people from bondage to the Egyptians. We have just seen how he spoke of his own death as an event that would free many others from slavery. In both instances we have a passage through the depths into new life—in other words, a "baptism"—and it would not be surprising if Jesus, with a mind steeped in the lore of his people's history, had seen a connection that even we do not find too obscure.

In any case, whether Jesus drew the parallel in his own human thinking or not, this much is clear. Without in any way forcing the evidence to yield more than it actually contains, we can see how Jesus' language about his "baptism" in death belongs to a family of symbols, in which water figures as at once a threat of death and a promise of new life. Jesus' death, as he understands it, follows the same rule of redemptive action as the Exodus, as Israel understood the latter event. Redemption comes when man puts himself wholly and unreservedly into God's hands and goes down into the threatening waters, to rise from their depths renewed and free.

No doubt there is a good deal of sheer mythology behind the water symbolism of the Bible. Even though the Old Testament writers are fiercely opposed to the religious conceptions of pagan mythology, their world remains in many respects the world of myth, and the depths of their sea are peopled by the frightful monsters of primitive imagination. But the really important fact is that the prophets and teachers of Israel have reshaped the ancient images into symbols of their own distinctive teaching. The fearsome inhabitants of the deep are now the creatures of the one true God.

> O Lord, how manifold are thy works! in wisdom hast thou made them all; the earth is full of thy riches.
> So is the great and wide sea also; wherein are things creeping innumerable, both small and great beasts.
> There go the ships, and there is that leviathan, whom thou hast made to take his pastime therein. Ps. 104:24-26

The sea itself may still be the great reservoir of chaotic and destructive forces, but those tremendous energies are now seen to be part of God's creation, ordered by his power to serve his purpose. The divine Wisdom presided over the making of the sea as of all else that exists.

> I was set up from everlasting, from the beginning,
> Or ever the earth was.
> When there were no depths, I was brought forth;
> When there were no fountains abounding with water. . . .
> When he established the heavens, I was there:
> When he set a circle upon the face of the deep,
> When he made firm the skies above,
> When the fountains of the deep became strong,
> When he gave to the sea its bound,
> That the waters should not transgress his commandment,
> When he marked out the foundations of the earth;
> Then I was by him, as a master workman.
> Prov. 8:23-30, ERV

In fact, the earth is built on the turbulent powers of the sea.

> The earth is the Lord's, and the fulness thereof;
> The world, and they that dwell therein.
> For he hath founded it upon the seas,
> And established it upon the floods.
>
> Ps. 24:1–2, ERV

It follows naturally that the deep waters should be the arena in which God acts to redeem and renew the works of his hands.

> Thou hast mightily delivered thy people, even the sons of Jacob and Joseph.
> The waters saw thee, O God, the waters saw thee, and were afraid; the depths also were troubled. . . .
> Thy way is in the sea, and thy paths in the great waters, and thy footsteps are not known.
> Thou leddest thy people like sheep, by the hand of Moses and Aaron.
>
> Ps. 77:15–20

The language may still be mythological, but the fundamental religious truth is clear. To go down into the waters is to submit to a remaking at the very foundation of our being. It is to run the ultimate risk for the sake of the ultimate reward—to let the old life be dissolved so that the new life can be born.

> The passage through the waters efficaciously signifies the return to a principle "prior to all forms," a "sort of chaotic totality of all possibilities," where an existence marked by certain qualities is dissolved into the undifferentiated, in order to rise to a new manner of being. . . . The dialectical link between the waters of Death and the waters of Life is so close that it is not possible to rise renewed from the wave unless we have suffered death in its bosom. . . . The waters both put to death and give new birth; they are an abyss where one is lost and a womb where one is reborn.

In other words, it is only through total and unconditional surrender to the power of God, which makes and breaks and remakes, that men can rise to their true place in the divine plan for the created world.

The "baptism" of Jesus is just such a surrender as this. He really goes down into the waters of death, letting go of life totally, completely, unreservedly. Willingly bearing the consequences of sin, he pays the price of the full and perfect service of God in a sinful world. He has joined our corrupted and distorted race to renew our humanity from within and bear it to its destiny beyond sin and death, and to accomplish his purpose he surrenders his own human flesh and blood in full and final obedience to his Father. He shares the natural human shrinking from death, the horror of letting go of natural life. But he is faithful to his own truth—the truth put so sharply to James and John and later enshrined in another great saying: "Unless a grain of wheat falls on the ground and dies, it remains just one grain. But if it dies, it yields a great harvest" (John 12:24). He goes through the gate of death—the very jaws of "hell," the realm of death—in order that our human nature, restored and transformed through him, may reach the goal for which God created it. He puts his perfect human life wholly in God's hands, beyond all human fears and human hopes. Only then, when in free and steadfast obedience he has immersed himself in the dark and turbulent waters, is he exalted by God's power and shown to his apostles as the "first-born from among the dead" (Col. 1:18), the source of new and eternal life for the people of God.

II

More than a quarter of a century after Jesus had spoken so challengingly of his own imminent "baptism," St. Paul was writing a letter to the Christians who lived in the capital of the Roman Empire. He too had to cope with a serious misunderstanding of the Gospel. Apparently some Christians were taking the line that the good news of salvation through the death and resurrection of Jesus Christ exempted them from all endeavor of their own. All that was expected of them was to acknowledge Christ's unique and complete work and then coast effortlessly into the destiny which Christ had won for them. Some of them may even have suggested that believers ought "to continue to sin to increase the spread of mercy" (Rom. 6:1)—to put it baldly, to give Christ more sins to atone for.

St. Paul was not at all hazy about the unique and final significance of Christ's work. He was fully convinced that mankind's eternal hope rested solely on Christ's atonement for sin and his victory over death. But he was no less certain that each believer in the crucified and risen Lord was called to die to sin and live for God, and that no one who ignored that call could hope for a share in Christ's victory. By our very entrance into the fellowship of believers, he told the Roman Christians, we commit ourselves to a decisive transformation of our lives.

Do you not know that all of us who have been baptized into union with Christ Jesus have been baptized into his death? Through baptism we have been buried with him in death, so that just as he was raised from the dead through the Father's glory, we too may live a new life. For if we have grown into union with him by undergoing a death like his, of course we shall do so by being raised to life like him, for we know that our old self was crucified with him, to do away with our sinful body, so that we might not be enslaved to sin any longer, for when a man is dead he is free from the claims of sin. If we have died with Christ, we believe that we shall also live with him, for we know that Christ, once raised from the dead, will never die again; death has no more hold on him. For when he died, he became once for all dead to sin; the life he now lives is a life in relation to God. So you also must think of yourselves as dead to sin but alive to God, through union with Christ Jesus. Rom. 6:3–11

This time it is perfectly obvious what is meant by "baptism." St. Paul is talking about a definite ritual act, the sacrament of Baptism by which from the beginning men have been initiated into the Christian community and the Christian life. Yet it would be a great mistake to confine our attention to the ritual act as such. For this particular action is not meaningful or effective in itself or because of the material element that is used in it. The rite of Baptism is a *sacrament,* a sacred sign, an effectual symbol of a holy reality. Just because it is a sacrament it points to something beyond itself, and its essential purpose is to relate those who celebrate it to that unseen something.

In the case of Baptism, the point of sacramental reference is easy enough to identify. The name itself is a sufficient clue. The ancient ceremony of baptism had symbolized death to an old form of existence and rebirth to a new. What the ritual imagery pictured has happened in solid fact in the saving acts of Jesus Christ. From now on the ritual act will be the sacrament of Baptism—a rite which retains all its ancient symbolic associations but which refers directly and properly to the real-life fulfillment of the old symbols. Even if St. Paul had not spelled out the connection between Christian Baptism and Christ's death and resurrection with such care, it would hardly be possible to miss the point. A "baptism" performed by believers in the unique redemptive power of the crucified and exalted Christ could not conceivably be anything but a representation of his true "baptism" on the cross. The real question is not what the sacrament of Baptism represents, but how it represents it. If we can answer that question, we shall come at least a little closer to understanding our relation both to the Gospel events and, through them, to the ultimate meaning of our lives.

The baptism of Jesus in Jordan by John the Baptizer is a good place to start looking for an answer. Apart from anything else, it happens to be one of the chief reasons for the existence of the Christian sacrament. Perhaps in some ways the Jewish practice of baptizing Gentile converts provided a more obvious precedent for Christian initiation, but Jesus' baptism by John, accompanied as it was by the Father's acknowledgment of his Son and the descent of the anointing Spirit, made a deep impression on the early Christian consciousness and might well have been enough to ensure the continuation of the rite in the Christian Church. At all events, no believer could enter the baptismal water without remembering that his Lord had been there before him.

We already know something of what Jesus' water baptism meant to him. The ritual act was a solemn prelude to his "baptism" on Calvary—a commitment to the redemptive task that lay before him and that would not be completed until he plunged into the deep waters of death. If Christian Baptism mirrors

Christ's baptism at John's hands, it must at least mean this: that baptized Christians are committed to the thoroughgoing imitation of their crucified Lord. By the fact of their Baptism, Christians are pledged to die to sin, to live in obedience, and in the end to accept their own death in trustful submission to the God who has raised Jesus from the dead. Whatever else Christian Baptism may be, it is nothing less than a promise of faithfulness in following Christ and a confession of faith in the almighty love which his resurrection reveals.

This much could be said even if the Christian sacrament were simply a repetition of John's baptism of repentance. But of course Christian Baptism is something far greater. John himself (we are told) said so:

> "After me there is coming one stronger than I am, one whose shoes I am not fit to stoop down and untie. I have baptized you in water, but he will baptize you in the holy Spirit."   Mark 1:7–8

Out of their fuller knowledge Christian believers must agree with him. The Christian sacrament is a symbol of Christ's flesh-and-blood "baptism," and it communicates the spiritual, supernatural fruits of his redemptive acts. In St. Paul's words, it is a Baptism "into union with Christ Jesus" (Rom. 6:3), crucified, buried, and gloriously risen. Through Christ's death and resurrection the ritual act of commitment and confession has become a real sacrament, a sign and instrument of union with Christ. In outward form it still reproduces his water baptism, but in inward reality it brings his true "baptism" to bear on human lives. When mortal and sinful man is baptized into Christ, he begins in that moment to "share his sufferings and even his death" and to "know him in the power of resurrection" (Phil. 3:10). It is not just that we promise to imitate Christ in his death and hope to imitate him in his resurrection. Our relation as Christians to the events of the Gospel is much closer than that. From the moment of our Christian initiation we begin to participate in Christ's suffering and in his glory—to die with him and to lay hold on eternal life in him.

I am not pretending that Christian Baptism instantaneously results in a natural death and a supernatural resurrection. There are too many baptized people walking around in the same old tired bodies for that notion to be very plausible. I am not even claiming that Christian Baptism immediately and infallibly produces a higher standard of moral living. The story of Christianity from its first days until now makes it only too obvious that the grace of Christ can be misused and resisted. What I am saying is that the sacrament of Baptism is a creative act of Christ in his Church; that through it he brings the cleansing power of his death and the renewing grace of his resurrection into our lives, to remake us in his likeness; that in it we can find the resources for a victorious struggle against sin and death. In Baptism the crucified and risen Lord comes into our hearts, to prepare us for a death and a resurrection like his own.

We are told that in moments of conflict and despair the stormy soul of Martin Luther again and again found rest in two words. *Baptizatus sum,* he would say to himself—I have been baptized, I am a baptized man. Every Christian can rightly take courage from those same words, because they succinctly state the ground of the Christian's ultimate hope. To understand the sacrament of Baptism is to know the mystery of Christ's own "baptism," in which he passed through death to eternal life. To receive the sacrament of Baptism is to be touched by eternity in time, as our lives are linked with the life of the crucified and exalted Christ. No power on earth—not even the power of bodily death itself— can destroy a hope built on such a foundation.

Baptizatus sum. Words of hope they certainly are—but words of challenge too. The sacrament of Baptism, given and received in time, is the pledge and seal of our destiny in eternity. But between the pledge and its fulfillment there lies the long highway of the Christian life, with all its opportunities and responsibilities and demands. The Christian message tells of the renewal of life, not of release from life, and the power of Christ's death and resurrection is to touch everything in every life. The foundation is firmly laid, and the end is irrevocably promised to all who build faithfully on that firm foundation, but here and now we have our building to do. The old hymn describes our position forthrightly.

A charge to keep I have,
A God to glorify;
A never-dying soul to save,
And fit it for the sky;
To serve the present age,
My calling to fulfill;—
O may it all my powers engage
To do my Master's will!

Arm me with jealous care,
As in thy sight to live;
And O! thy servant, Lord, prepare
A strict account to give:
Help me to watch and pray,
And on thyself rely;
Assured if I my trust betray,
I shall for ever die.

One or two of Charles Wesley's phrases may have an old-fashioned ring, but the point he makes is as valid today as it was two centuries ago. There is no way of evading the obligations and the discipline of the Christian life. When we are baptized, and in our Baptism are joined to the crucified and risen Christ, our lives are redirected toward their true goal, but unless we step out boldly and willingly in faith and obedience we have no real hope of completing our appointed journey.

Baptizatus sum. Christ has died and Christ has been raised from death. By his death and resurrection Christ has converted the blank wall of death into the open gate of eternal life. In our Baptism our faces have been set toward that open gate. When we come to die, will we pass through it to our true destiny? The answer is in our hands now.

CHAPTER 5

REPRESENTATION: HOLY COMMUNION

> The Lamb's high banquet we await
> In snow-white robes of royal state;
> And now, the Red Sea's channel past,
> To Christ our Prince we sing at last.
>
> Upon the altar of the cross
> His body hath redeemed our loss;
> And tasting of his roseate blood
> Our life is hid with him in God.
>
> That Paschal eve God's arm was bared;
> The devastating angel spared:
> By strength of hand our hosts went free
> From Pharaoh's ruthless tyranny.
>
> Now Christ our Paschal Lamb is slain,
> The Lamb of God that knows no stain;
> The true oblation offered here,
> Our own unleavened bread sincere.
> —Latin hymn, seventh century

I

We began the last chapter by listening to Jesus as he talked to his little band of disciples on their final pilgrimage to Jerusalem. He was trying to make them understand what the outcome of their journey must inevitably be. As we listened, and reflected on what we heard, we were able to form a pretty clear picture of his deliberate intention in making the journey. He was going to Jerusalem to undergo the "baptism" to which he had solemnly dedicated himself at the outset of his ministry. That ministry was now drawing to its close; he believed that God's time was ripe;

and he was going up to the holy city to die. ". . . I must go on," he said, "today and tomorrow and the next day, for it is not right for a prophet to die outside Jerusalem" (Luke 13:33).

In spite of repeated warnings, his followers had no such clear perception of God's strange purpose. They were full of vague fears for the future, but they seem to have paid very little attention to what Jesus had to tell them. Probably, like most people in a crisis, they preferred to seek refuge in a familiar routine. They were planning to celebrate the Passover together in Jerusalem, and they did not mean to look any further if they could help it. If God had other plans for them, and if this Passover was to change their lives almost beyond recognition, all that was still hidden in a future which they were none too anxious to penetrate.

Jesus went to Jerusalem to lay down his life, his disciples to celebrate a holiday. At first glance, their respective intentions seem to have nothing in common. Yet in reality Jesus was not completely out of sympathy with his disciples, for he too was going to Jerusalem to keep the Passover. He even seems to have shared the longing of his little flock to enjoy another Paschal meal together. "I have greatly desired," he told them, "to eat this Passover supper with you before I suffer" (Luke 22:15). But something beyond this natural human desire drew him still more strongly to the feast. He was moved by the awareness of a mysterious affinity between the Paschal celebration and his own approaching end. "I tell you," he went on after the sentence I have just quoted, "I will never eat one again until it reaches its fulfilment in the Kingdom of God" (Luke 22:16). And a little later, we are told, he added, "The Son of Man is going his way, as it has been decreed" (Luke 22:22). Plainly, the Passover and his own fate are closely linked in his mind.

Just why should the Passover have meant so much to Jesus (as well as to his followers) in the closing days of his life? To find an answer, we must begin by looking at the Paschal feast itself. As Jesus knew it, it was the celebration of the Exodus from captivity in Egypt—Israel's "Independence Day." Probably, like the story of the Exodus as the Bible tells it, the feast of the Passover was rooted in older traditions that are now lost to us. Certain of its features suggest that it may originally have been an agricultural festival. But for the Hebrew scriptures and the later Jewish tradition it is the greatest of all historical celebrations, the festival of Israel's deliverance from serfdom and its remaking as God's holy people. The Book of Exodus confidently ascribes that meaning to it.

> Moses said unto the people, Remember this day, in which ye came out from Egypt, out of the house of bondage; for by strength of hand the Lord brought you out from this place: there shall no leavened bread be eaten. This day ye go forth in the month Abib. And it shall be, when the Lord shall bring thee into the land . . . which he sware unto thy fathers to give thee, a land flowing with milk and honey, that thou shalt keep this service in this month. . . . And thou shalt tell thy son in that day, saying, It is because of that which the Lord did for me when I came forth out of Egypt. And it shall be for a sign unto thee upon thy hand, and for a memorial between thine eyes, that the law of the Lord may be in thy mouth: for with a strong hand hath the Lord brought thee out of Egypt.
>
> Exod. 13:3–9, ERV

The real origin of the name of the feast is at least as obscure as the ultimate origin of the feast itself, but the conventional accounts connect it in one way or another with the Exodus. The more or less official explanation derives the name from one of the grimmer details of the departure from Egypt. According to the Old Testament narrative, when Moses and Aaron had failed to get any action from Pharaoh on the liberation of Israel, in spite of the series of nine plagues, a tenth and most frightful plague was inflicted on Egypt, and all the firstborn of men and of cattle in the whole country died in one night. The Israelite young alone escaped the destroyer, because in accordance with God's command the doors of their houses were marked with the blood of the Paschal lamb. From this immunity to the "Tenth Plague" the festival takes its name.

> It shall come to pass, when your children shall say unto you, What

mean ye by this service? that ye shall say, It is the sacrifice of the Lord's passover, for that he passed over the houses of the children of Israel in Egypt, when he smote the Egyptians, and delivered our houses.

Exod. 12:26–27, ERV

Another strand of the Judeo-Christian tradition offers an explanation which shifts the emphasis without altering the essential character of the commemoration. The word "Passover," it is suggested, refers to the climactic episode of the Exodus, namely, the "passage" of Israel through the Red Sea. Early Christian writers took quite readily to this rendering of the term, as many instances show.

> *Post transitum maris rubri*
> *Christo canamus principi.*

So runs the ancient hymn.

> After the "Passover" of the Red Sea
> Let us sing to Christ our Chief.

No doubt the picture is complicated here by the fact that *transitus* ("passing through" or "crossing") refers at once to the Exodus and to Christian Baptism. Nonetheless, the lines are a good example of a deep-rooted tradition, for which the Passover was the celebration of the Red Sea passage.

Perhaps even these few details have given us something of the flavor of the feast. It was a great festival, rich with complex associations, that drew Jesus and his disciples to Jerusalem in that springtime so long ago. To the patriot it told of the heroic adventure that had made Israel a people and planted it in the land of promise. To the believer it spoke of the God whose strong hand claimed Israel for his service and would finally accomplish his full purpose. For every child of Israel it was a time warm with memories and shining with hopes. At Passover, as at no other time, the holy nation stood revealed in all the wonder and the dignity of its calling.

> I was glad when they said unto me, We will go into the house of the Lord.
> Our feet shall stand in thy gates, O Jerusalem.

Jerusalem is built as a city that is at unity in itself.
For thither the tribes go up, even the tribes of the Lord, to testify unto
Israel, to give thanks unto the Name of the Lord.   Ps. 122:1–4

Even the most unimaginative pilgrim must have felt a little of the
poet's emotion as he set out for the historic capital of his nation
and his faith to keep the great feast of deliverance.

After all this build-up it may at first sight seem sheer anti-
climax to remark that it is not at all clear that Jesus and his disciples ever did manage to celebrate that fateful Passover together.
Yet in sober truth the evidence is inconclusive. On the one hand,
the Synoptic Gospels (Matthew, Mark, and Luke) say quite plainly
that the Last Supper, on what we should call Maundy Thursday
evening, was the Passover meal. On the other hand, according to
the Fourth Gospel Jesus died on the cross at about the time when
the lambs were being slaughtered for the Paschal supper. As a
general rule, modern historians prefer the Synoptists to St. John
when a choice must be made. In this case, however, probably the
majority of competent scholars think that a number of details
preserved by the Synoptic Gospels do not fit in with the idea that
the Last Supper was the Passover, and they are prepared to follow
the Fourth Gospel against the inconsistencies of the others. I am
inclined to think that the argument against the Synoptists is not
as strong as much current scholarship supposes and that greater
allowance should be made for the possibility that St. John has
adjusted his time scheme in order to accentuate a theological
point, but I must admit that these suspicions do not add up to a
solution. Perhaps it never will be possible to decide the question
conclusively. Fortunately, it does not really matter to Christian
theology whether it is decided or not. The Last Supper may have
been the Paschal meal, or alternatively Christ's death may have
coincided with the killing of the Paschal victims, but in one way
or the other the meaningful connection between the Passover,
with all that it stands for, and the Gospel events is secured.

Whether the Last Supper was in fact the Paschal meal or
something quite different, what Jesus himself said and did at the

table makes the connection unmistakably clear. St. Paul's narrative of the Supper, which is probably our earliest written evidence of what went on, brings out the point well enough.

For I myself received from the Lord the account that I passed on to you, that the Lord Jesus the night he was betrayed took some bread and gave thanks for it and then broke it in pieces, saying, "This is my body which takes your place. Do this in memory of me." He took the cup, too, after supper, in the same way, saying, "This cup is the new agreement ratified by my blood. Whenever you drink it, do so in memory of me." For until the Lord comes back, every time you eat this bread and drink from the cup, you proclaim his death.   1 Cor. 11:23-26

Along with several other significant themes, the Exodus motif stands out. The phrase "the new agreement ratified by my blood" points back directly to the event which revealed the purpose of the Exodus, God's making an "agreement" or "covenant" with the ransomed people at Sinai.

Two Old Testament passages will help us to fill in the background of Jesus' words. The first is the story of the making of the covenant at Sinai. It tells how Moses, when he had written down all God's instructions, had sacrifices offered and sprinkled sacrificial blood on the altar.

And he took the book of the covenant, and read in the audience of the people: and they said, All that the Lord hath spoken will we do, and be obedient. And Moses took the blood, and sprinkled it on the people, and said, Behold the blood of the covenant, which the Lord hath made with you upon all these conditions.   Exod. 24:7-8, ERV

The second passage is an oracle of the great prophet Jeremiah, which brings a new promise from God to Israel. God intends to bring his people into a more intimate fellowship with himself than they have ever known.

Behold, the days come, saith the Lord, that I will make a new covenant with the house of Israel, and with the house of Judah: not according to the covenant that I made with their fathers in the day that I took them by the hand to bring them out of the land of Egypt; which my covenant they brake, although I was a husband unto them, saith the Lord. But this is the covenant that I will make with the house of Israel after those days, saith the Lord: I will put my law in their inward parts, and in their heart will I write it; and I will be their God, and they shall be my people. And they shall teach no more every man his neighbor, and every man his brother, saying, Know the Lord; for they shall all know me, from the least of them unto the greatest of them, saith the Lord: for I will forgive their iniquity, and their sin will I remember no more. Jer. 31:31–34, ERV

Against the background of these texts, what Jesus is saying is not too hard to understand. With the help of a different image— the symbol of the "covenant"—he is making the familiar and fundamental point that his redemptive death and resurrection are the new and more perfect Exodus, the final deliverance from sin and death, of which the " 'Passover' of the Red Sea" was the real but remote anticipation. When he dies during the Paschal celebration, he is completing the divine plan in which the Passover festival and all that it stands for are a significant but transitory phase. At Sinai liberated Israel was called to fulfill its divine mission; in Christ's death and resurrection liberated mankind was called to attain its divine destiny.

So far so good. But so far we have accounted for only part of the phrase that Jesus used. "This cup," he said, "is the new agreement ratified by my blood." As we have seen, he meant to compare the old and imperfect covenant which secured the promised land to Israel with the new and perfect covenant which secures eternal life to believers. But that was not quite all that he meant. According to biblical ways of thinking, a covenant was ratified by the offering of sacrifice. The Exodus narrative tells us how the covenant of Sinai was sealed with sacrifices and the sprinkling of sacrificial blood. Quite naturally, then, when Jesus compared the covenants he also compared the offerings which ratified them. The new and perfect covenant, he declared, would be ratified by the perfect sacrifice, which was to be nothing less than the outpouring of his lifeblood in unconditional obedience to the will of God.

Earlier in this book we looked carefully at the notion of sacrifice and tried to see what light it could shed on the meaning of

Jesus' death. There is no need for us to cover that ground again. But we can profitably linger for a moment over the point that Jesus was making when he contrasted his sacrificial death with the sacrifices of the old covenant, because it touches the heart of our Christian life. He was saying, in effect, that the only approach to true and perfect communion with God was through his redeeming death. Under the new and perfect covenant there could be no sacrifice and no priesthood but his own, because his offering was the sole authentic act of worship, the one true sacrifice of praise and thanksgiving and propitiation and supplication. Once his full, perfect, and sufficient offering had been made, there would be no place in God's world for animal sacrifices or for any of the imperfect approaches to God which men had devised and God had graciously used to promote his own loving purpose. In the past men had gone up to Jerusalem year after year to sacrifice and eat the Paschal lamb in remembrance of Israel's deliverance from Egypt. Now they must go out into every city and every land to proclaim the Lamb of God, once slain to take away the sin of the world.

Jesus' own words spoke explicitly of the "new agreement." Thus it was to the contrast between the covenant of Sinai and the covenant of Calvary that his disciples' attention was immediately directed. But the Church was quick to draw the fullest conclusions from his teaching and to see in him and his redeeming work the fulfillment of every feature of Israel's great deliverance. Since Jesus had in fact been crucified at the time of the Passover, and since he himself had evidently seen in that fact something more than superficial coincidence, the predictable outcome of this development was an emphasis on the forms of the Paschal feast as symbolic clues to the meaning of what Jesus had done for man. Less than three decades after the crucifixion, St. Paul could use the image of Christ the true Paschal Lamb as a talking point in a moral exhortation to a Greek-speaking congregation in a pagan city.

Do you not know that a little yeast will affect all the dough? You must

clean out the old yeast and become fresh dough, free from the old as you
really are. For our Passover lamb is already sacrificed; it is Christ himself.
So let us keep the festival, not with old yeast nor with the yeast of vice
and wickedness, but with the unleavened bread of purity and truth.

1 Cor. 5:6–8

In this Paschal form, Jesus' teaching about sacrifice became a
Christian commonplace. His death was the true Paschal sacrifice,
the event to which all Passovers pointed. Once seen in that perspective, it was readily recognized as the reality of which all
human attempts at worship are but dim shadows, the sole ground
of man's approach to the God of all life and joy. From the first
days of Christianity Jesus' sacrifice has stood alone in the eyes of
Christian faith, and Christian devotion has hailed it as unique in
its worth and perfect in its power.

> Paschal Lamb, thine offering, finished
> Once for all when thou wast slain,
> In its fulness undiminished
> Shall for evermore remain,
> Alleluia,
> Cleansing souls from every stain.

II

The self-oblation of Jesus Christ is the one and only true and
eternally valid offering of worship from mankind to God. In the
Christian scheme of things there is no need and no room for another offering over and above the sacrifice of Christ. And yet the
New Testament writers can repeatedly urge on Christian believers the inescapable duty of making their own personal offering
to God. Each believer in the crucified and risen Christ must
somehow make his own living and dying into a genuine sacrifice,
offered up in union with the Lord's death. "I appeal to you,
therefore, brothers," St. Paul writes, "by this mercy of God, to
offer your bodies in a living sacrifice that will be holy and acceptable to God; that is your rational worship" (Rom. 12:1). A few
years later, near the end of half a lifetime's meditation on the

Gospel, he can even find the courage to ascribe some kind of redemptive value to his own experience of suffering. ". . . I am
glad," he tells the members of one of his churches, "to be suffering in your interest, and I am making up in my own person what
is lacking in Christ's sufferings for the church, which is his body"
(Col. 1:24). Christ has indeed made the one perfect offering of
worship and atonement, but believers in him are mysteriously
drawn to share in his sacrifice.

Part of the secret of our participation in Christ's sacrifice can
be found in what we have already learned about our Baptism into
Christian fellowship. When we were considering the work of
Christ, approaching it through the symbol of baptism, we discovered that Christ's "baptism" in death and resurrection was a
foundation on which we had to build our own life and death.
The foundation, we learned, is indispensable; apart from God's
action in Jesus Christ we have no hope of realizing the meaning
of our lives. But we also learned that unless we set ourselves to the
task of building on the sure foundation our hope in Christ must
necessarily remain empty and unfulfilled. In other words: Christ
has died and Christ is risen; Christ has touched our mortal flesh
with the immortal power of his death and resurrection; in laying
his consecrating hand upon us Christ has given us a real and vital
hope of dying in union with his death and rising in the likeness of
his resurrection—but it is only by the daily dying of self-surrender
and the daily resurrection of renewed obedience that we can
claim that hope for our very own.

All this amounts to saying that we share in Christ's sacrifice by
right of our Baptism and in fulfillment of the inherent demand of
our Baptism. It is true that only Christ's holy life is an offering
worthy to be laid down before the holy God and that only his
atoning death breaks through the barrier erected by sin between
man and his Maker. But the fact of our Baptism into his death
at once enables and constrains us to join ourselves to his self-
offering.

For just as the body is one and yet has many parts, and all the parts of the body, many as they are, form one body, so it is with Christ. For we have all—Jews or Greeks, slaves or free men—been baptized in one spirit to form one body, and we have all been saturated with one Spirit.

1 Cor. 12:12–13

If that is what our Baptism into union with Christ Jesus means, then it follows inescapably that we can and must share in the sacrifice of his body. When he offered his body on the "altar of the cross," in anticipation he offered all those who were to be incorporated into him. Now that we have become one body with him, we can claim and we must take our part in his offering. In Christ's death and resurrection man has approached God and has found acceptance; now all who believe in Christ must approach God in union with him, offering up their living and their dying, and looking for final acceptance into eternal life. If the whole scheme of ritual sacrifice has so completely lost its meaning through Christ's work that we find it hard to imagine how it ever made sense to anyone, we are not to conclude that we have been exempted from offering sacrifice. The right conclusion is that at last we can really offer ourselves in sacrifice, because we make our offering in union with our crucified and risen Saviour and it is hallowed and uplifted by his offering.

Baptism is something that is done to us; sacrifice is something that we do. No doubt, if we happen to be baptized as adults, we can be said to submit ourselves to Baptism, but in the action itself we remain objects, whereas in the act of sacrifice we are subjects. We are baptized, but we offer sacrifice. It seems to me that this contrast raises a basic question about the manner of our union with Christ in his self-offering. Our Baptism both entitles and summons us to offer ourselves with Christ; of that there can be no doubt. But in itself Baptism is a sacrament or "sacred sign" of our entrance into union with the crucified and risen Lord—not a sacrament of our action in union with him. In other words, it is the sign of our incorporation into Christ, not of our self-offering as his members. Has God, then, not given us a sacred sign of our Christian sacrifice, a holy action in which day by day the countless thoughts and words and deeds that make up the fabric of our lives can be offered to our heavenly Father through Christ his Son?

The answer, of course, is that he has done just that in bidding us celebrate the Eucharist or Lord's Supper or Holy Communion or Mass or Liturgy; it does not matter which historic title we use, so long as it puts us in mind of the holy action—the second of the two great sacred signs of the Gospel of Christ, which stand first among the Church's sacramental actions. The Eucharist is the solemn rite which Jesus performed at the Last Supper and ordained to be repeated in remembrance of his sacrifice. It is celebrated with outward elements—bread and wine—which in the history of man's approach to God have repeatedly been set forth and poured out in sacrifice, but it is not just one more ritual sacrifice. In its outward order it is closely akin to the sacred meals that have meant so much in the religious life of Judaism, but it is not just another sacred meal. Its inward reality sharply distinguishes it from all that has gone before.

> Types and shadows have their ending,
> For the newer rite is here.

The Eucharist is a sacrament of Christ—the divinely appointed symbol of the one true and perfect sacrifice and the instrument through which, by God's grace, that offering and our offering are made one.

Scholars have advanced theories, compounded of information and imagination in varying proportions, to explain the origin of the Eucharist, but their quest has not proved particularly rewarding. The Lord's Supper, as we find it in the New Testament and in the later Church, cannot be readily identified with any earlier rite, and its meaning cannot be directly derived from such pre-Christian antecedents as we can trace. No doubt Christians have often spoken loosely of the Eucharist as the "Christian Passover," but their reason was that they saw in it the sacrament of Christ, the true Paschal Lamb. Thus St. Thomas Aquinas could write, in one of his great doctrinal poems:

> Lo! the new King's table gracing,
> This new Passover of blessing
>   Hath fulfilled the elder rite.

But he went on to show how the essential meaning of the Eucharist depends on Christ himself.

> Lo! the angels' food is given
> To the pilgrim who hath striven;
> See the children's bread from heaven,
>   Which to dogs may not be cast;
>
> Truth the ancient types fulfilling,
> Isaac bound, a victim willing,
> Paschal lamb, its lifeblood spilling,
>   Manna sent in ages past.

Externally, the Lord's Supper obviously belongs to the same tradition of sacred meals as the Passover supper, but its unique significance was given to it by Jesus Christ, when in one and the same act he declared the purpose of his death and instituted the Eucharist. "This is my body which takes your place. . . . This cup is the new agreement ratified by my blood." In these words Jesus announced his imminent death and spelled out its sacrificial meaning. "Do this in memory of me." The same actions that foretold his death are to be for the Church the means of communion with him in his sacrifice.

This "memory" and this communion are much more than a mental remembering and an emotional sympathy. In the Lord's Supper, the sacrament of Christ's sacrifice, Christians really enter into the offering of the Head of the Church. Again and again, spreading forth on God's table the mysterious signs which Christ has blessed, we represent to God the true sacrifice of the new and perfect covenant, praying that as we adhere more and more closely to it we may draw nearer and nearer to our destiny in God. "The Lord's suffering," an early father of the Church tells us, "is the sacrifice we offer." The sacrifice is Christ's, and yet, by his gift, we make it our own. As we have seen, the sacrifice of the Lord's suffering included in anticipation all those who were to be grafted into his body, and in the Lord's Supper we take our due place in his offering. With humble spirit and contrite mind we bring to the altar the simple tokens of our loving obedience, and in fulfillment of his promise Christ takes them and blesses them, making them the sacred sign of his own pure sacrifice of love. Together with him, we represent and set forth his sacrifice—that sacrifice which so strangely and wonderfully includes our poor selves. Then, in the act of communion, we renew our union with him, seeking to draw the spirit and power of his sacrifice more and more deeply into the earthly, fleshly reality of our lives.

Some lines from a modern English hymn say all this about as well as it can be said. In them the Church very simply and very humbly asks the Father to accept her offering for Christ's sake.

> We offer to thee of thine own,
> Ourselves and all that we can bring,
> In bread and cup before thee shown,
> Our universal offering.
>
> All that we have we bring to thee,
> Yet all is naught when all is done,
> Save that in it thy love can see
> The sacrifice of thy dear Son.
>
> By his command, in bread and cup
> His body and his blood we plead;
> What on the cross he offered up
> Is here our sacrifice indeed.
>
> For all thy gifts of life and grace,
> Here we thy servants humbly pray
> That thou wouldst look upon the face
> Of thine anointed Son today.

This sacrament of sacrifice, instituted by Jesus Christ on the night before he suffered for our redemption, has been the center of Christian worship and life from the beginning. We are told that the first converts to Christianity, won by St. Peter's preaching on the day of Pentecost, "devoted themselves to the teaching and the society of the apostles, *the breaking of bread,* and the prayers" (Acts 2:42, italics added), and that day by day, after taking part in the Temple worship, those first Jewish Christians "broke their bread together in their homes" (Acts 2:46). All our accounts of early Church life make it plain that this example was followed as the faith spread and the community grew, and that the Eucharist was the chief and characteristic feature of Christian worship. In the age of the great persecutions of the Church by pagan Rome, multitudes of Christians repeatedly risked their liberty and their lives in order to take their part in this sacred action, and the Church took great pains to carry the consecrated gifts even into the prisons to believers suffering for their faith. We hear of one imprisoned priest who managed despite his chains to celebrate the Eucharist, using his own body for the altar. Wherever Christians were found, and whatever the conditions under which they lived, it was second nature to them to offer up their joys and sorrows in communion with the saving Victim of Calvary.

As the centuries went by and the Church won the allegiance of many nations and in turn found herself deeply involved in their lives and problems, she did not always succeed in preserving the integrity of her worship. In the vast, sprawling society that Christendom had become, only too many Christians came with dim understanding and feeble devotion to their common worship, and Christian congregations no longer manifested the warm and eager piety of the primitive eucharistic fellowships. In Western Christendom in particular, the combination of unsatisfactory practice and questionable interpretation brought on crisis after crisis. Misleading assertions and extravagant denials followed one another in a vicious spiral, and the world was treated to the paradoxical and scandalous spectacle of Christians quarreling among themselves over the mystery of the one body and the one loaf. Even today, four centuries after the climactic episodes of the conflict, there is probably no other area of disagreement in which divided Christians cherish such weird misconceptions of one another's teaching.

Yet we cannot dismiss all these failures and conflicts as a total loss to Christianity. Deplorable as their controversial manners and morals have often been, at least Christians have been guided by a sound instinct in supposing that the Lord's Supper mattered greatly to the Church and that profound disagreements about its true meaning could not be taken lightly. The Lord's Supper, after all, is the heart of Christian worship and life, and believers must always be deeply concerned to know its real nature and to use it rightly. If the Church's eucharistic worship is corrupted and her eucharistic teaching distorted, nothing else in her life can be really sound. In Christ's plan for his Church, the sacrament of his sacrifice is the place where his people's vital contact with the realities of the Gospel is repeatedly renewed, and if their approach to that holy action goes wrong their whole common life in Christ will inevitably suffer.

The sacrament of Christ's sacrifice is the place where Christians again and again renew their vital contact with the realities of the Gospel. With that reminder our reflections on the Eucharist may fittingly close. In the Eucharist we represent Christ's sacrifice, offered on the cross and sealed with the divine acceptance in the resurrection. In representing Christ's sacrifice sacramentally, we commit ourselves to a life of sacrificial love and obedience in union with him and after his perfect example. In committing ourselves more and more wholeheartedly to sacrificial living in constant communion with our crucified Lord we advance step by step toward the gate of life, which his death and resurrection have opened to all believers. In a word, in the Lord's Supper Christ gives us the key to our life's true and final meaning, by drawing us into fellowship with himself, our suffering and glorious Saviour.

> Salvation's Giver, Christ the only Son,
> By his dear cross and blood the victory won.
> Offered was he for greatest and for least:
> Himself the Victim, and himself the Priest.
>
> Victims were offered by the law of old,
> That, in a type, celestial mysteries told.

He, Ransomer from death and Light from shade,
Giveth his holy grace his saints to aid.

Approach ye then with faithful hearts sincere,
And take the safeguard of salvation here.
He that in this world rules his saints and shields
To all believers life eternal yields.

PART THREE
SACRED SEASONS

CHAPTER 6

COMMEMORATION: SUNDAY

> This is the day the Lord hath made,
>   He calls the hours his own;
> Let heaven rejoice, let earth be glad,
>   And praise surround the throne.
>
> Today he rose and left the dead,
>   And Satan's empire fell;
> Today the saints his triumph spread,
>   And all his wonders tell.
>   —Isaac Watts

It is Sunday morning—any Sunday morning—in the year of our Lord nineteen hundred and sixty-two. The turning of the great globe brings continent after continent into the sunlight and one by one the church bells ring out, just as they have rung ever since Christians first were free to build churches and hang bells in their steeples. This year of grace is very much like every other year in the Church's history. She is hard pressed by the enemies of her creed and her way of life, and in many of her own children the pulse of faith and hope and charity can hardly be felt. But in spite of everything, the bells are still ringing this morning, and in every country where the Gospel is known Christians are gathering, as they have gathered on almost a hundred thousand Sundays, to give thanks for God's mighty and merciful acts. Today is Sunday, and the call to worship is insistent.

O give thanks unto the Lord, for he is gracious: because his mercy endureth for ever. . . .
Yea, let them now that fear the Lord confess, that his mercy endureth for ever.

I called upon the Lord in trouble; and the Lord heard me at large.

The Lord is on my side; I will not fear what man doeth unto me. . . .

The Lord is my strength, and my song; and is become my salvation.

The voice of joy and health is in the dwellings of the righteous; the right hand of the Lord bringeth mighty things to pass. . . .

I shall not die, but live, and declare the works of the Lord. . . .

This is the Lord's doing, and it is marvellous in our eyes.

This is the day which the Lord hath made; we will rejoice and be glad in it.   Ps. 118

"This is the day which the Lord hath made." For over nineteen centuries the "Lord's Day" has been the strong recurring accent in the rhythm of Christian living. In his report of St. Paul's missionary journeys, St. Luke can already refer to Sunday observance as a matter of course. "On the first day of the week," he tells us, "when we had met for the breaking of bread, Paul addressed them" (Acts 20:7). Later and fuller evidence simply confirms and elaborates this early hint. Our first detailed accounts of early Church life make it clear that Sunday worship was generally recognized as one of the marks of Christian discipleship. From the first century onward, the first day of the week has been the Christians' special day—the day which in their eyes is above all others "the day which the Lord hath made."

As everyone knows, a weekly holy day is not a Christian invention. Like the Christian sacraments, the Christian calendar has a prehistory in Judaism, and the broad likeness between Sunday and the Sabbath is obvious enough. For many centuries before Christ, the Sabbath was one of the fundamental institutions of the religion of Israel. Its essential rule, supplemented by a brief explanation, was laid down in the famous "Ten Words":

Remember the sabbath day, to keep it holy. Six days shalt thou labour, and do all thy work: but the seventh day is a sabbath unto the Lord thy God: in it thou shalt not do any work, thou, nor thy son, nor thy daughter, thy manservant, nor thy maidservant, nor thy cattle, nor thy stranger that is within thy gates: for in six days the Lord made heaven and earth, the sea, and all that in them is, and rested the seventh day: wherefore the Lord blessed the sabbath day, and hallowed it.   Exod. 20:8–11, ERV

As the years passed, legal commentary applied the basic rule to just about every conceivable situation in public and domestic life, so that by the time of Jesus the sacred rest of the Sabbath was thoroughly fenced off from secular intrusion. While Jesus himself was actively critical of the niggling attitude of certain experts in religious law, who seemed to him to have lost sight of the real point of the Sabbath in a maze of technicalities, he did conform to the chief conventions of Sabbath observance, including habitual attendance at the synagogue, and a casual spectator might well have thought that this example would secure for the Sabbath a permanent place in the rising Christian community.

But in fact the Sabbath contributed little if anything to Christian practice, beyond the general notion of a weekly holy day. No doubt the first Christians kept up the Sabbath observance that had been bred in their Jewish bones, but when the Church began to spread into the Gentile world it quickly became apparent that the Sabbath had no real meaning for Christians in general. Along with other Old Testament customs, it might be used as a symbol of Christ and his work, but otherwise the life had gone out of it. St. Paul bluntly tells Christian believers where they stand.

So no one can call you to account for what you eat or drink, or do about annual or monthly feasts or Sabbaths. That was all only the shadow of something that was to follow; the reality is found in Christ.   Col. 2:16–17

As for Sunday, its essential idea is quite independent of the Sabbath. The Sabbath and its rules belonged to the old order of things; Sunday grows out of the new. Sabbath observance was a commandment of the law; Sunday observance is a proclamation of the Gospel. The Sabbath was a mere foreshadowing of the eternal life that God was to give us in Christ; Sunday has an almost sacramental quality as a sign of what God has now done. Sunday expresses the reality that is found in Christ. Sunday is the "Lord's Day."

The "Lord's Day"—just what does that title imply? First and foremost, the Lord's Day is the day of the Lord's resurrection. It was in the resurrection that the purpose of Christ's life and death was accomplished. It was through the resurrection that the

Son who took the form of a servant and became obedient unto death entered into his Kingdom and was made known as Lord. The day of Christ's resurrection was his day of fulfillment and exaltation and revelation. Surely it was natural and supremely fitting for the Church to mark it for all time as the "Lord's Day" and hallow it week by week by breaking bread in memory of the Lord's sacrifice.

It was the stupendous fact of Christ's resurrection that first set Sunday apart from all other days as the Lord's Day. Put to death on Good Friday, "on the third day he was raised from the dead" (1 Cor. 15:4). ". . . very early on the first day of the week they went to the tomb, when the sun had just risen" (Mark 16:2). The keeping of the Lord's Day is firmly rooted in the soil of historical reality, and every first day of the week looks back to that "first day after the Sabbath, . . . [when] Jesus came in and stood among them and said to them, 'Peace be with you!'" (John 20:19). But while the phrase "the first day of the week" speaks directly of a particular day when a particular event happened, it has symbolic overtones which Christian ears can scarcely fail to hear. To minds familiar with the imagery of the Bible, "the first day of the week" is above all the first day of the symbolic week of God's creation of the world. The Church fathers could hardly make enough of the coincidence of images, in which they found a clue to the place of Christ's resurrection in God's purpose. On the first day of the creation God made the light shine out from the darkness of the still formless world. On the first day of the resurrection God brought the Light of eternal life out of the darkness of the grave. As the early Christians saw it, the light of time prefigured the Light of eternity and the Light of eternity fulfilled the promise of the light of time. The first day of the creation saw the universe of creatures begin to emerge from God's hands; the first day of the resurrection saw created manhood raised up in glory, the first fruits of the new creation. On the first day of the creation God's transcendent purpose for man was foreshadowed; on the first day of the resurrection that same purpose was realized.

Seen in this perspective, the celebration of the Lord's Day on the first day of the week is a sign of the inauguration of a new creation in Christ. The Lord's Day tells us that the work of the "six days," far from completing God's creative plan or exhausting his creative power, was just a beginning, and that in Christ's resurrection God has done a new thing to bring his human creatures to their destiny beyond time and death. The teachers of the early Church were fully aware of this witness borne by the Lord's Day to the novelty of the Gospel, and they were determined that no one should miss the point. If necessary, they would even improve on the symbolism of the "first day of the week." It was clear enough to them, but perhaps it could be made clearer still. The first day of the week came round every seven days, as another weekly cycle began; could the parallelism of the first day of creation and the first day of the resurrection really bring out all the new, creative force of God's action in Jesus Christ? The new creation is not simply a return to the beginning, a fresh start for the world of nature. The new creation is a new and fresh and supernatural act of the Creator, which emancipates man from the natural limits of creaturely life and takes him up into eternal communion with God. In order to symbolize this truth more adequately, the Church fathers began to speak of Sunday as the "eighth day." Sunday is much more than the sign of another cycle begun; Sunday must be seen as the token of a novel act of God's creative power. The Lord's Day is the "eighth day," the image of eternal life beyond the seven days of time.

Perhaps some of us find all this number symbolism strange, or even childish, but what it stands for is permanently valid for Christians. Sunday is not just a ritual occasion, let alone a day arbitrarily hedged in by quaint taboos. Sunday is one of the great historic symbols of the crucified and risen Christ. Sunday is the Lord's Day—not in any exclusive sense, as if all days did not belong to the King of ages, but because on this day the Lord Christ rose from death. Sunday is the Lord's Day, because on this day God's purpose for mankind was accomplished in Christ. Sunday is the Lord's Day, because on this day God inaugurated his new creation. Sunday is a sign of what God has done in Christ and a token of what God will do in us. Sunday is a glimpse through the gate of death—a glimpse of our final destiny in God.

The Christian calendar began with the observance of the Lord's Day, and through the centuries the long line of Sundays has formed the backbone of the Christian year. The tradition is worth keeping up, today and tomorrow and always, because the message of Sunday is the good news that gives meaning to all our times. "This is the day which the Lord hath made"—the day of joy and gladness, the symbol of our faith and our hope in Christ, the pledge of eternal life.

CHAPTER 7

CELEBRATION: EASTER

'Tis the spring of souls today;
  Christ hath burst his prison,
And from three days' sleep in death
  As a Sun hath risen;
All the winter of our sins,
  Long and dark, is flying
From his light, to whom we give
  Laud and praise undying.

Now the queen of seasons, bright
  With the day of splendour,
With the royal Feast of feasts,
  Comes its joy to render;
Comes to glad Jerusalem,
  Who with true affection
Welcomes in unwearied strains
  Jesu's resurrection.
                    —St. John of Damascus

"And note, that every Parishioner shall communicate at the least three times in the year, of which Easter to be one." This direction may not be much of an example of the striking English prose for which *The Book of Common Prayer* of the Church of England is so famous, but it embodies a great and venerable tradition, whose influence can still be traced from one end of Christendom to the other. Apart from the weekly observance of the Lord's Day, the annual feast of the resurrection is the most ancient feature of the Christian calendar, and all through the Christian centuries it has stood out as the great holy day of the Church year. In the Mediterranean world of the first century, in medieval Europe, in the young Christian communities of the Americas and the still younger churches of Africa and the Orient —in short, wherever the Gospel has been heard—the Easter festival is the crown of the year's worship. In outward appearance the Paschal vigil of fifth-century Rome, the "all-night service" of the Orthodox East, the Easter morning Eucharist of an Anglican congregation in Canada or Australia, the "sunrise services" and splendid musical offerings of American Protestantism, and the hundred other ways of keeping "the Feast" are very different, but they all reflect the common Christian conviction that the celebration of Easter must dominate the Church's worship because the message of Easter is the foundation of Christianity.

We can best grasp the essential meaning of Easter by getting as close as we can to its roots in the faith and life of the primitive Christian community. As the early Church knew it, the Easter festival was nothing less than the comprehensive celebration of the Gospel of redemption through Christ. Its outward observance consisted of a day of fasting, a night watch (during which, from an early date, Baptism was administered), and the eucharistic memorial of Christ's sacrifice. Its purpose was to draw the whole Church into union with Jesus Christ in his death and resurrection. There was no "Good Friday" set over against "Easter Sunday"; no separation between death and resurrection either in liturgical action or in theological idea; no hint of cleavage in the great mystery of redemption. There could be no festival of Christ's death by itself, and no festival of his resurrection apart from his death, because the two events were episodes in one tremendous divine action. The death of Christ was the offering of a sacrifice; the resurrection of Christ was the divine acceptance of the same sacrifice. Or better—because the imagery brings out more clearly the continuity of God's redemptive action in Christ— in his death and resurrection Christ passed through the waters of destruction and dissolution to the land of renewed and transformed life. The Gospel of our salvation is one indivisible story, and in the early Christian Easter the one indivisible Gospel is celebrated as one story in the night vigil, in Baptism, in the Eucharist.

The early Christians called their great feast of redemption the "Pascha," and in their minds it was obviously connected with the Jewish feast of redemption, the "Pascha" or Passover. As we already know, the New Testament writers looked on Jesus' death as the offering of the true Paschal Lamb, and the Christian Easter may well have begun as a continuation of the Jewish festival with a fuller and deeper meaning. Even in the latter half of the second century we find the Christians of Asia Minor clinging tenaciously to the custom of celebrating Easter on the same day as the Passover, and it is conceivable that they were right in ascribing their rule to an apostolic tradition. Since the Quartodecimans, or "Fourteenthers"—so named because they insisted on keeping Easter on the fourteenth day of the Jewish month Nisan, regardless of the day of the week—and their opponents understood the "Pascha" in the same way, their dispute can hardly have been anything but a conflict of traditional loyalties, and on that level the Quartodecimans may have had the better case.

On the other hand, in terms of Christian symbolism the alternative tradition of a Sunday Easter was stronger, and by the beginning of the third century it seems to have won out everywhere. Given the universally recognized meaning of the "Pascha" as the celebration of Christ's death and resurrection, it is hard to see what else could have happened. The rhythm of the Christian year was already determined by a distinctively Christian commemoration of the same events, the weekly Lord's Day, and in the long run the assimilation of the yearly celebration to the fundamental weekly observance was inevitable. While the "Pascha" may have originated quite independently of Sunday, its essential theme coincided with the essential theme of the Lord's Day, and a natural attraction eventually drew the two holy days into an indissoluble unity.

Once definitively established as a Sunday festival, Easter more and more took on the character of the "Sunday of Sundays." All the symbolic associations that had clustered around Sunday as the day of the resurrection were reclaimed for the festival of the resurrection, and in its light shone more brightly. To borrow the language of the old Roman Christians, if Sunday was kept as the *perennitas*, the repeated Lord's Day that week by week hallowed the year, Easter was honored as the *solemnitas*, the unique Lord's Day that crowned the hallowed year. Easter was celebrated as the "Feast of feasts," the Lord's Day above all other Lord's Days, the great symbolic day of fulfillment, the glorious sign of the new creation in the risen Christ. "This is the day which the Lord hath made"; if those words could rightly be applied to Sunday, they belonged with far better right to Easter. In fact, the early Christians' sense of the presence of the glorified Christ on the day of his resurrection was so vivid that many of them expected that the final "Day of the Lord"—the glorious manifestation of Christ that was to bring human history to an end—would take place while the Church was celebrating the Easter festival.

Inevitably, the "Feast of feasts" and "Sunday of Sundays" will be a great event in the life of any congregation. As it approaches interest will quicken, and people will spare no effort to pay fitting honor to such a solemn occasion. The church building will be as clean and beautiful as human hands can make it; the furniture of the Lord's table will be polished until it gleams and sparkles; the music of the Easter services will be carefully chosen and tirelessly rehearsed. All that is as it should be—but it is not enough. The Christian calendar was not devised merely to provide congregations with a series of impressive liturgical experiences. The Christian year was shaped to bring Christians nearer to Christ. Since human beings are creatures of flesh and blood, they are profoundly affected by sights and sounds, by patterns of action and rhythms of time. In her feasts and fasts, the Christian Church meets these strange creatures where they are, using signs and seasons to bring the Gospel of Christ into their lives. What the sacred signs of the Gospel—Baptism and the Eucharist—show forth in unvarying simplicity is spelled out day by day and week by week in symbolic action as well as in word, until the whole life of believers is touched by the whole Gospel. Seen in this light, a Christian festival clearly demands much more than a purely external and mechanical preparation. Time must be found for prayer and for reflection on the mystery of the Gospel. Minds and hearts must be opened wide to receive God's truth and grace. It is not enough to prepare the outward means of keeping the feast; believers must prepare themselves to live the feast.

Other Christian festivals exhibit some particular aspect or presupposition or consequence of the Gospel of Christ, but the "Feast of feasts" declares the whole Gospel at once. At the season of the year when in historical fact Christ died and rose again, the Church's liturgy calls all Christian people to a concentrated, corporate recollection of the saving events. Looking back in faith to what God has done and forward in hope to what he has promised to do, the Church gives him thanks for the wonder of his new creation and proclaims that wonder to the world as the key to life's meaning. In accordance with a custom as old as Easter itself, the Church celebrates the Lord's Supper, calling every believer to take his full part in showing forth Christ's sacrifice. In accordance with a custom so ancient that we cannot tell when it began, the Church administers Baptism, drawing more human lives into union with the crucified and risen Christ and calling every believer to a truer and fuller living of the baptized life. To put it in one sentence, Easter is the great Lord's Day of the new creation, the great eucharistic day of corporate communion in Christ's sacrifice, the great baptismal day of death and resurrection with Christ.

Supremely rich in its meaning, the Easter festival is supremely searching in its demands. Every year of our Christian lives, Easter gives us a new opportunity to live our way into a closer, deeper fellowship with our suffering and glorious Lord. That kind of experience is not something that we can casually drop in on; it must itself be lived into by thought and prayer and self-discipline.

That is where Lent comes in.

CHAPTER 8

PREPARATION: LENT

Alleluia we deserve not
  Here to chant for evermore:
Alleluia our transgressions
  Make us for a while give o'er;
For the holy time is coming,
  Bidding us our sins deplore.

Trinity of endless glory,
  Hear thy people as they cry;
Grant us all to keep thy Easter
  In our home beyond the sky;
There to thee our Alleluia
  Singing everlastingly.
          —Latin hymn, before eleventh century

In the Northern Hemisphere, where it was first observed, Lent comes with the spring. At one time or another, millions of Christians must have wondered why. In northern latitudes, at any rate, February and March are not the most promising time for a great spiritual effort. Winter seems to have been going on forever, and the first faint signs of spring come and go with little apparent effect. People are tired—tired of the cold and the darkness, tired of rain and sleet and snow and ice, tired of aches and coughs and sneezes. Comfort and relaxation were never more needed. But what does the Church do to mark this low point of the year? She announces a season of fasting and prayer, and invites us to cut down on food and drink, to forget about luxuries and entertainments, to spend more time on our knees. Why (we ask ourselves more or less seriously) does she do it? Does she really have to impose so many extra burdens on weary mortals?

114

The answer, of course, is that the Church is not just trying to be difficult. Lent comes when it does because Easter falls when it does. Lent is what it is because the "Feast of feasts" is what it is. Lent is not an arbitrary summons to endure hardness for the sake of enduring hardness; Lent is a serious preparation for the Easter festival, with all its rich meaning. Lent is a way of growing into Easter, a way of making the truth of Easter part of our lives.

We have already learned something of the purpose of Easter. Easter is meant to be a profound Christian experience for all who take part in it—a time of wholehearted identification with Christ in his death and resurrection. Easter is a call to surrender ourselves to death with the Lord Jesus and a symbol and pledge of resurrection to eternal life through the Lord Jesus. Easter is a foreshadowing of salvation, an image of our final destiny.

If Easter is all these things (and more), it is not surprising that from the beginning Christians should have been expected to work hard at preparing themselves for it. Even the earliest Paschal celebration began with a day of rigorous fasting, and the strict fast was soon extended to two days (Friday and Saturday before Easter). Before long the period of bodily self-discipline was enlarged into something that we can appropriately call "Lent." As early as the third century, Alexandria (and probably Rome as well) kept all of "Holy Week" as a fast. By the end of the century Rome was experimenting with a more ambitious three-week fast, beginning right after what we now call the fourth Sunday in Lent. (The explanation of this unusual Lent seems to be that the period between March 1, then the Roman New Year's Day, and March 22, the earliest possible date for Easter, was precisely three weeks.) At some point in the fourth century both Alexandria and Rome introduced a six-week preparation for Easter, commencing on our first Sunday in Lent. Finally, after trying out one or two other reckonings, the Roman Church settled on "Ash Wednesday" as the opening of the fast, and the Lenten calendar as we know it throughout Western Christendom was complete. Similar developments took place in other parts of the Christian world, and by the fifth century the expanded Lent could fairly be called a universal Christian institution.

What ideas underlay this complex but consistent evolution? The six-week Lent in its various forms obviously reflects an interest in Christ's own fast of forty days in the desert, but Christians had been keeping Lent for a long time before they undertook a literal imitation of Christ's fast. The original and fundamental idea of Lent has to do with a more profound imitation of Christ. In its essence the Lenten fast was and is an attempt to die to self in order to live in Christ. As a description of what we ourselves make of Lent, that sentence may have an ironical ring. An austere priest once remarked rather bitterly, after lunching with an eminent prelate on a day of abstinence, that there was "a lobster-salad element in the good Cardinal's character," and I suspect that the same could be said of very many modern Christians. But the Christians who made and molded Lent were altogether in earnest about what they were doing, and they fasted hard enough to make their Lent a real and prolonged act of self-denial in union with Christ's own sacrifice.

In one of his famous sermons St. Leo the Great tells us that Lent is nothing less than a preparation of the whole Christian people for salvation. If the real Lent is what I have just said it is, we can at least begin to see what St. Leo is getting at. Rightly kept, Lent does much more than prepare us to celebrate a festival, important as that festival is. Insofar as the experience of Lenten living really impresses Christ's suffering and death more deeply on our minds and hearts, Lent helps to fit us for the destiny which Easter prefigures. By spending a segment of our time in single-minded communion with our dying Lord, we begin to make all our time into a preparation for our death to time and our resurrection to eternity.

In the same summary of the meaning of Lent, St. Leo points out that the Lenten observance is also a preparation of the "chosen ones" for their Baptism during the Paschal vigil. Once Easter was established as the normal time for administering Baptism, the final corporate preparation of candidates for Baptism invariably coincided with the Church's season of preparation for Easter. In the course of time, as the Lenten liturgies of Christendom show quite clearly, the process of preparation for Baptism contributed more than a little to the shaping of the whole Church's Lent. What we might call the "general" and "special" purposes of Lent became so closely interwoven in the actual Lenten observance that the whole Christian people found themselves not only preparing to celebrate Easter as the "Feast of feasts," but also reliving their preparation for Baptism.

The end result, of course, was a reinforcement of the primary meaning of Lent. The presence of the catechumens was a forceful reminder of the reality for which Lent stood. In St. Leo's own fifth century, as in any other, it was all too easy to fall into the habit of treating Lent and Easter as a piece of solemn play-acting. The constant renewal of the memory of Baptism would obviously be a strong corrective of any such inclination. No Christian who had repeatedly been made to think through the significance of his own Baptism could fail to apprehend the real demand of Lent and the real promise of Easter.

As St. Leo describes it, Lent includes still another important feature. Lent, he says, is a preparation of the "penitents" for their reconciliation on the Thursday before Easter. In the early Church it was customary for those who had confessed grave moral lapses to be put through a period of exacting discipline before they were restored to communion by absolution. Since Easter was the great feast of the Christian year, exclusion from the Paschal Eucharist would be an especially heavy penalty. Consequently, penitents who were ready for reconciliation were allowed to pass through the final stages of their penance during Lent and to receive their absolution just before the Paschal celebration began. As time went on, this particular penitential use of Lent affected the entire Church's observance of the season. To cite just one example, in the Roman liturgy the symbolic imposition of ashes on "Ash Wednesday," which had originated as part of the symbolic "expulsion" of the penitents at the outset of their Lenten discipline, became a solemn consecration of the whole community at the beginning of the Lenten fast.

Once again, the use of Lent for a special purpose helped to bring out its basic meaning. We know that Lent is meant to be an experience of dying with Christ. But just what does "dying with Christ" involve? The answer lies in the meaning of Christ's own death. "Christ died for our sins" (1 Cor. 15:3). Christ died to break the power of sin, and to die with him means to die to sin. That lesson is already taught in the opening event of our Christian life. St. Paul asks:

> When we have died to sin, how can we live in it any longer? Do you not know that all of us who have been baptized into union with Christ Jesus have been baptized into his death? Through baptism we have been buried with him in death, so that just as he was raised from the dead through the Father's glory, we too may live a new life.   Rom. 6:2–4

As St. Paul's argument suggests, however, the event of Baptism is the beginning, not the end, of the Christian's deadly warfare against sin. Baptism is a real act of grace against sin, but the battle between grace and sin will go on as long as man lives. Sin is not merely a flaw on the surface of human life. The distorting and corrupting effects of sin reach into the depths of man's being. The temptation to sin is insidious and incessant, and no one is wholly immune to it. Again and again believers fall short of the full demand of the new life in Christ. Again and again they must be recalled to their baptismal dignity; again and again, in earnest penitence, they must die to sin and rise to righteousness. In this world as it actually is, it is only through such a constantly renewed death to sin that Christians can meet the demand and realize the promise of their Baptism. Dying with Christ involves a repeated dying to sin through repentance. If Lent is to be an authentic Christian experience of dying with Christ, one of its essential aspects will therefore be a summons to truer and deeper penitence. Insofar as the early Church's system of discipline helped to fix this penitential meaning of Lent more firmly in the

Christian mind and in the practice of the Church, it made an enduring contribution to every Christian's Lenten observance.

Through the centuries Christian rules of fasting have repeatedly been changed to meet changing conditions. The elaborate program of preparation for Baptism disappeared when the Church's first great age of missionary expansion came to an end. Public penance has for the most part been either replaced by private confession or simply given up. In short, the outward appearance of Lent has been drastically transformed between St. Leo's day and our own.

Yet its fundamental meaning remains the same. Lent is still the time when, as we prepare to keep the Easter festival, we reach through it to the ultimate destiny which it symbolizes. Lent is still the time when Christians as a body renew their baptismal union with the crucified and risen Christ. Lent is still the time when we learn to die more completely to sin so that we may live more completely for God.

CHAPTER 9

CONCENTRATION: FASTING

> The glory of these forty days
> We celebrate with songs of praise;
> For Christ, by whom all things were made
> Himself has fasted and has prayed.
>
> Alone and fasting Moses saw
> The loving God who gave the law;
> And to Elijah, fasting, came
> The steeds and chariots of flame.
>
> So Daniel trained his mystic sight,
> Delivered from the lions' might;
> And John, the Bridegroom's friend, became
> The herald of Messiah's name.
>
> Then grant us, Lord, like them to be
> Full oft in fast and prayer with thee;
> Our spirits strengthen with thy grace,
> And give us joy to see thy face.
>   —Ascribed to St. Gregory the Great

Everyone who has any interest at all in Lent is sure of one fact—that Lent is a time for giving up things. Even a young child will ask his small friends, as a matter of course, "What are you giving up for Lent?" He may be a little vague about our Lord's warning against publicizing our self-denials, but he is quite definite about the need for self-denial, and he takes it for granted that Lent is a suitable time to practice it. In his experience, that is how right-minded people feel.

This notion of Lent is sound enough, of course, as far as it goes. Whatever fuller meanings it may have taken on, Lent did in fact begin quite simply as a preparatory fast before the Paschal vigil and the Paschal Eucharist. In the ancient world it was widely held that fasting was an especially effective way of preparing for a sacred action, and quite early in Christian history the custom grew up of keeping a fast in preparation for the Holy Communion. The initial Lenten observance was part of the same pattern; indeed, it might quite aptly be described as the fast before the Easter Communion. But if Lent is basically a fast, then it necessarily involves "giving up," because to fast is certainly to do without or give up something.

So far so good; our well-brought-up little boy is evidently on the right track. If we intend to keep Lent, we must be ready to give up something. But why (we cannot help going on to ask) would anyone suppose that giving up something—more precisely, doing without food and drink—was the proper approach to a sacred action? To put it crudely, what is so good about getting hungry?

Obviously the Christian practice of fasting is not to be explained on the basis of ancient taboos. Christians could not seriously believe that the presence of food in the stomach was spiritually defiling, or that certain foods were intrinsically impure. The recorded words of Jesus were far too definite:

And he said to them,
"Have not even you any understanding then? Do you not see that nothing that goes into a man from outside can pollute him, since it does not go into his heart but into his stomach and then is disposed of?" So he declared all food clean.   Mark 7:18–19

Still less can Christian fasting be linked with the kind of dualistic hostility toward the material world that led the medieval Albigenses to regard suicide by fasting as the supreme religious act. In the New Testament itself, dualistic notions about eating and drinking were definitively repudiated. "For everything God has created is good," one typical statement runs, "and nothing need be refused, provided it is accepted with thanksgiving" (1 Tim. 4:4).

It is clear that genuine Christian fasting has nothing to do either with dietary taboos or with dualistic heresies. Where then should we look for its real motives? I think that the true basis of the Christian practice of fasting is unquestionably to be found in the biblical doctrine of God and creation. The biblical world view implies just that evaluation of the creature which Christian fasting presupposes. For the Bible, the world of things is God's creation. Because God made it, it is good and can rightly be enjoyed. But two conditions must always be observed. In the first place, because creatures belong to God, they must be used responsibly in obedience to his will. In the second place, because creatures are God's handiwork, and not God, they must never be allowed to hinder man from paying due attention to God. As even a quick glance will show, these two principles are reflected quite accurately in the Christian use of fasting.

The influence of the biblical principle of responsibility in the use of God's creatures can plainly be seen in the Christian emphasis on almsgiving as a weighty motive for fasting. From very early days, Christian fasting has been intimately associated with almsgiving. Again and again the Church fathers stress the point that strict fasting makes generous almsgiving possible. If I discipline my own use of creatures, I can share God's good gifts more liberally with others whose need is greater than my own. Nor is such a distribution of material goods merely a casual by-product of Christian fasting. Fasting is meant to be an aid to almsgiving. One of the Christian's essential aims in curbing his own luxury is to free himself for acts of charity, and if he fails to perform those acts his fasting is an empty form.

From all this it is quite apparent that the first of our two biblical principles regarding the use of creatures has strongly influenced the Christian conception of fasting. The influence of the principle of giving the Creator his due is no less obvious and even more significant. If the Christian tradition connects fasting with almsgiving, it links it still more closely with prayer. The great spiritual writers repeatedly tell us that fasting liberates man for prayer. When I pray, I lift up my mind to God and fix my heart on him as the ultimate concern of my existence. When I fast, by detaching myself from creaturely goods I free myself to turn more recollectedly and urgently to God. Fasting thus helps me to concentrate and intensify my prayer. Nor is this relation of Christian fasting to prayer merely incidental. If fasting is intended to be an aid to almsgiving, it is meant above all else to be an aid to prayer. The Christian's supreme aim in fasting is to foster prayerful concentration on the ultimate meaning of his life, and a fast that fails to lead to prayer is not a Christian fast at all. Some lines attributed to Gregory the Great put the essential idea quite perfectly:

> Give us the self-control that springs
> From discipline of outward things,
> That fasting inward secretly
> The soul may purely dwell with thee.

Christian fasting obviously has a solid basis in the biblical teaching about God and his creatures. As we might expect, it also has deep roots in the biblical history. The supreme example, of course, was provided by Jesus Christ himself in the long fast that followed his baptism by John in the Jordan. We are told:

The spirit immediately drove him out into the desert. And he remained in the desert for forty days, and Satan tried to tempt him there; and he was among the wild animals; but the angels waited on him.   Mark 1:12–13

Other examples, however, helped to shape Christian attitudes and customs. Two episodes from the Old Testament made a particularly strong impression on early Christian readers, partly because the personalities involved in them were great symbolic figures, and partly because in some respects they closely resembled Christ's great fast.

In the first of these episodes the central figure is Moses. As the Book of Exodus tells the story, the great covenant has just been ratified at Sinai, and Moses and Aaron and the elders of Israel have gone up into the mountain to eat and drink before God. Now God speaks to Moses:

Come up to me into the mount, and be there: and I will give thee the

> tables of stone, and the law and the commandment, which I have written, that thou mayest teach them.   Exod. 24:12, ERV

In obedience to God's order, Moses leaves Aaron and the elders, goes up toward the summit of the mountain, and disappears into the cloud that covers it.

> And the appearance of the glory of the Lord was like devouring fire on the top of the mount in the eyes of the children of Israel. And Moses entered into the midst of the cloud, and went up into the mount: and Moses was in the mount forty days and forty nights. Exod. 24:17–18, ERV

The hero of the second episode is Elijah—"Mr. Prophecy," we might call him, in view of his place in Jewish and Christian symbolism. As the story opens, he has just won his spectacular contest with the prophets of Baal on Mount Carmel, and the losers have been massacred. Since Queen Jezebel is not taking the loss of her pet prophets lightly, Elijah decides to go off to the desert and hide. Once he gets there, however, he is sunk in gloom, and asks God to take away his life. Almost immediately, remarkable things begin to happen. In the morning Elijah wakes up to find biscuits and water beside him, supplied by an angel.

> And the angel of the Lord came again the second time, and touched him, and said, Arise and eat, because the journey is too great for thee. And he arose, and did eat and drink, and went in the strength of that food forty days and forty nights unto Horeb the mount of God. And he came thither unto a cave, and lodged there; and, behold, the word of the Lord came to him, and he said unto him, What doest thou here, Elijah?
> 1 Kings 19:7–9, ERV

Then comes the revelation of God's power and God's will—not in the wind, not in the earthquake, not in the fire, but in the "still small voice." His courage restored, Elijah is sent back to Israel to complete his prophetic mission.

The Gospel, the law, the prophets—in their various ways all three stories seem to tell the same story. Jesus began his ministry with a fast of forty days in the desert. He watched with God; he suffered the pains of hunger; he underwent temptation. For nearly six weeks he cut himself off from human contacts and human pleasures, and fixed his attention on God and on God's will for his life. Then he came back into the world, fully prepared to begin his work of redemption. Centuries before him, according to the traditions of his people, the great lawgiver and the great prophet had anticipated his experience. Like him they had retreated from human society into remote places, to spend forty days and forty nights with God. Like him they had endured loneliness and hardship. Like him they had returned from solitude fully determined and ready to carry out God's purpose. It is not surprising that the early Christians should have sought and found a common lesson in the three stories, and that their imagination should have made the most of every similarity, including the fact that each episode had filled a period of "forty days."

We already know that Christianity has consistently treated fasting as at once an exercise in the right use of creatures and an effort at concentration of mind and heart on the divine Creator. These ideas of fasting are securely based on the biblical doctrine of God and creation. But from the great historical exemplars of fasting the Church derived a further idea, which has given sharper definition to the concept of concentration on God. In each of the three classical instances, fasting had been a preface to a mighty act of God. Moses had fasted, and had received "the two tables of the testimony, tables of stone, written with the finger of God" (Exod. 31:18, ERV). Elijah had fasted, and had experienced a great manifestation of God, which sent him back, encouraged and enlightened, to his prophetic calling. Our Lord Jesus Christ had fasted, and had gone forth from his fast to live and die and rise again in completion of the law and the prophets. The Church fathers did not find it too hard to draw their conclusion. Fasting (they decided) is above all an approach to the redeeming God—an approach evidently approved by God himself. When Moses and Elijah fasted, they prepared themselves to play their part in the drama of redemption. When Jesus fasted, he prepared himself to die and rise again for man's redemption. When Christians fast, they prepare themselves to receive the divine gift of redemption.

In the early Christian mind the "forty days and forty nights" of the three typical fasts somehow came to symbolize the meaning of fasting as a preparation for redemption. No doubt "forty days" was basically nothing more than an idiomatic expression for "a long time." In the biblical narrative, however, the number forty does keep reappearing in crucial situations, and it was natural for men who were intrigued by number symbolism to try to make something out of the coincidence. Moses' sojourn on Sinai, Elijah's journey to Horeb, and the fast kept by Jesus in the desert were all described as forty days long. Israel's wanderings in the wilderness went on for forty years. According to St. Luke's account, at any rate, forty days elapsed between Christ's resurrection from death and his ascension into heavenly glory. Against the background of these stories, read as the early Church read them, to keep a fast for forty days was to relate it, deliberately and explicitly, to the story of redemption.

Consequently, when we keep our Lenten fast of forty days, we are observing a fast that is clearly marked as an act of preparation for redemption. Of course, the fast of forty days does in fact imitate Christ's own fast more or less exactly, and many Christians have never seen anything more in it than that. But the real point of our Lenten "forty days" does not lie in a mere chronological imitation of our Lord's fast. The point is rather that we are putting our own self-denial into the same redemptive pattern to which Christ's fast belongs. In keeping Lent, we turn in faith and hope to our redeeming Lord, emptying our hands of everything else so that they may be ready to take his gift of full salvation.

CHAPTER 10

ILLUMINATION: INSTRUCTION

Christ, whose glory fills the skies,
  Christ, the true, the only Light,
Sun of Righteousness, arise,
  Triumph o'er the shades of night;
Dayspring from on high, be near;
Daystar, in my heart appear.

Dark and cheerless is the morn
  Unaccompanied by thee;
Joyless is the day's return,
  Till thy mercy's beams I see;
Till they inward light impart,
Glad my eyes and warm my heart.

Visit then this soul of mine,
  Pierce the gloom of sin and grief;
Fill me, Radiancy Divine,
  Scatter all my unbelief;
More and more thyself display,
Shining to the perfect day.
    —Charles Wesley

In the paintings of the Roman catacombs and the decorations of ancient baptisteries, three scenes very often appear. In the first scene, Jesus is sitting beside a well, talking to a woman. In the second scene, he is anointing a blind man's eyes with clay and sending him to wash in a pool. In the third scene, he is standing beside an open tomb, from which a shrouded figure is emerging.

The three scenes are not very hard to identify. All three represent incidents described in the Gospel of St. John. The first incident is Jesus' conversation with the Samaritan woman beside Jacob's Well at Sychar. The second is his healing of a blind man by putting clay on his eyes and sending him to wash in the Pool of Siloam. The third is his raising of Lazarus of Bethany from the grave. The three episodes are all full of symbolic meaning, which St. John's dialogue brings out very clearly, and it is not surprising to find that they were favorite themes with ancient Christian artists.

There was a special reason, however, for including these scenes in the decorations of baptisteries, or baptismal chapels. The symbolism of the three incidents seemed to the early Church to bear directly on the Christian sacrament of Baptism, and all of them occupied a conspicuous place in the scheme of prebaptismal instruction. In Rome, for example, they provided the themes for the three Sunday "scrutinies"—the solemn services of exorcism, blessing, and instruction which at one time were held on the three Sundays preceding Palm Sunday. On successive Sundays the Roman catechumens (and the whole Church with them) heard Jesus offer "living water" to the Samaritan woman, saw him disclose himself as the "light of the world" by curing blindness, and watched him raise the dead to life. From these three stories the "chosen ones" were expected to gain a new understanding of what it meant to confess Jesus Christ as Lord and Saviour and to receive Baptism into his death.

The first story, which the Roman candidates for Baptism will have heard on the third Sunday in Lent, is a lively story, marked by rather pointed irony. Jesus and his disciples are traveling through Samaria, and one day around noon they find themselves near a town called Sychar. Jesus is tired, and he sits down by Jacob's Well while his disciples go shopping for food in the town. A Samaritan woman appears with her pitcher, and Jesus asks for a drink. She expresses surprise, because he is obviously Jewish and Jews ordinarily segregate themselves from Samaritans. Jesus replies:

> "If you knew what God has to give, and who it is that said to you, 'Give me a drink,' you would have asked him, and he would have given you living water."						John 4:10

The woman apparently takes offense, and asks Jesus how he

expects to get water out of the well and if he thinks that he is a greater man than her ancestor Jacob. Jesus answers indirectly:

"Anyone who drinks this water will be thirsty again, but anyone who drinks the water that I will give him will never be thirsty, but the water that I will give him will become a spring of water within him, bubbling up for eternal life." John 4:14

The woman still misses the point. "Give me this water, sir," she says, "so that I may never be thirsty, nor have to come all this way to draw water" (John 4:15). Jesus tells her to go home and fetch her husband. When she answers that she has no husband, Jesus proceeds to display considerable knowledge of her personal history. The woman sees a chance to turn the conversation into an argument about the claims of the Jerusalem temple. She can tell (she says) that Jesus is a prophet; perhaps he would like to say a word on this disputed point. Jesus' response goes far beyond anything that she has dreamed of:

"Believe me, the time is coming when you will worship the Father neither on this mountain nor at Jerusalem. You worship something you know nothing about; we know what we worship, for salvation comes from the Jews. But a time is coming—it is already here!—when the true worshipers will worship the Father in spirit and sincerity, for the Father wants such worshipers. God is spirit, and his worshipers must worship him in spirit and in sincerity." John 4:21–24

The woman says nothing, except that all these problems will be solved when the Messiah comes. Jesus replies, "I who am talking to you am he!" (John 4:26).

At this point the conversation is interrupted by the return of the disciples. The woman rushes off to the town and says to everyone she meets, "Come, here is a man who has told me everything I ever did! Do you suppose he is the Christ?" (John 4:29). A good many of the townspeople are impressed by her story, and when they reach the well they invite Jesus to stay in the town— which he does for a couple of days.

And a great many more believed because of what he said, and they said to the woman,

"It is no longer because of your statement that we believe, for we have heard him ourselves, and we know that he is really the Savior of the world." John 4:41–42

As the catechumens listened—most of them probably for the first time—to this story, they must have been deeply impressed and moved. In so many ways it was their own story. Some of them at least, when they first came in contact with the Christian revelation, had been no more perceptive than the Samaritan woman was in the first moments of her conversation with Jesus. Most of them had probably spent a fair amount of time asking questions very much like "Do you suppose he is the Christ?" For all of them the moment had eventually come when they could sincerely and happily confess Jesus Christ as the Saviour of the world. Now they were about to enter the waters of Baptism, there to receive from him the "living water" of his Spirit.

On the fourth Sunday in Lent, a week closer to their Baptism, our catechumens came back to hear the second story. Its setting is a long debate between Jesus and the Jews, which in St. John's narrative leads into the final crisis of Jesus' ministry. Jesus has said, "I am the light of the world. Whoever follows me will not have to walk in darkness but will have the light of life" (John 8:12). This assertion has touched off a violent argument, and Jesus has even been threatened with stoning. Now our story begins.

As he passed along, he saw a man who had been blind from his birth. His disciples asked him,

"Master, for whose sin was this man born blind? For his own, or for that of his parents?"

Jesus answered,

"It was neither for his own sin nor for that of his parents, but to let what God can do be illustrated in his case. We must carry on the work of him who has sent me while the daylight lasts. Night is coming, when no one can do any work. As long as I am in the world, I am a light for the world."

As he said this he spat on the ground and made clay with the saliva, and he put the clay on the man's eyes, and said to him,

"Go and wash them in the Pool of Siloam"—a name which means One who has been sent. So he went and washed them, and went home able to see. John 9:1–7

The cure brings on another long argument. The patient himself, his parents, his neighbors, and a group of Pharisees are all drawn into it. Is this really the same man who was blind? What has actually happened to him? Is it Jesus who has cured him? What does that prove anyhow? Is Jesus even a good man? In the end, the man whom Jesus has healed finds himself shut out of the synagogue.

> Jesus learned that they had excluded him, and he found the man and said to him,
> "Do you believe in the Son of Man?"
> The man answered,
> "Who is he, sir? Tell me, so that I may believe in him."
> Jesus said to him,
> "You have seen him already, and it is he who is now talking to you."
> He said,
> "I believe, sir!" and he fell on his knees before him.   John 9:35–38

Once again, the story must have spoken to the condition of the candidates for Baptism. They too had been called out of darkness into God's marvelous light. They had been shown where the true and ultimate meaning of their lives lay. They had discovered in Jesus Christ the Redeemer through whom (and through whom alone) that meaning could be attained. Now they were on their way to union with him in the sacred sign of Baptism. The story of each and every one of them could be summed up in the blind man's words, "All I know is that I was blind before and now I can see" (John 9:25).

A week later, on the fifth Sunday in Lent, the Roman catechumens came to the third Sunday "scrutiny" and heard the third of our stories. When the story begins, Jesus and his disciples have gone to stay in the country east of the Jordan, in order to escape from the Jerusalem authorities. Jesus learns that his friend Lazarus, who lives in Bethany, near Jerusalem, is sick, and after a couple of days he suggests returning to Judea. When the disciples object, he adds, "Our friend Lazarus has fallen asleep, but I am going there to wake him" (John 11:11). But the disciples can still see no reason for making the dangerous trip. After all (they argue), if Lazarus is sleeping he is obviously getting better. Finally Jesus has to tell them bluntly, "Lazarus is dead." Then he goes on, "and for your sake I am glad that I was not there, so that you may learn to believe in me. But let us go to him" (John 11:15).

As Jesus approaches Bethany, Lazarus' sister Martha comes out to meet him.

Martha said to Jesus,
"Master, if you had been here, my brother would not have died! Even now I know that anything you ask God for, he will give you."
    Jesus said to her,
"Your brother will rise."
    Martha said to him,
"I know that he will rise at the resurrection, on the Last Day."
    Jesus said to her,
"I myself am Resurrection and Life. He who believes in me will live on, even if he dies, and no one who is alive and believes in me will ever die. Do you believe that?"
    She said to him,
"Yes, Master, I do indeed believe that you are the Christ, the Son of God, who was to come into the world."   John 11:21–27

After Martha's confession of faith, events move quickly. Jesus goes straight to Lazarus' tomb, while Martha goes home to fetch her sister Mary. When Jesus sees Mary weeping he is moved and begins to show signs of his own deep distress. Many of the bystanders sympathize with him, but others are critical. "Could not this man," they ask, "who opened the eyes of that blind man, have kept Lazarus from dying?" (John 11:37). Still greatly disturbed, Jesus goes right up to the cave-tomb and orders the stone to be taken away from its mouth. Martha objects. Lazarus died four days ago; the soul has finally gone away from the body; nothing can do any good now. But Jesus insists, and the stone is moved. Jesus prays for a moment, and then shouts, "Lazarus, come out!" "The dead man came out," St. John concludes, "bound hand and foot with wrappings, and with his face muffled in a handkerchief. Jesus said to them, 'Unbind him and let him go'" (John 11:44).

Three sentences that come just before the climax of the story sum up its essential message for the candidates for Baptism.

Jesus said,
  "Move the stone away."
  The dead man's sister, Martha, said to him,
  "Master, by this time he is decaying, for he has been dead four days."
  Jesus said to her,
  "Have I not promised you that if you will believe in me you will see the glory of God?"   John 11:39–40

Decay, faith, glory—those three words mark out the path along which the catechumens are moving. They were born into a world of decay, a world reeking with the corruption of sin and doomed to the corruption of death. But they have come to confess Jesus as their redeeming Lord, and from him they are learning the lessons of holiness and hope. Soon, baptized into union with him, they will begin to taste the wonder and the power of the age to come.

The three "scrutinies" whose themes we have just been considering are typical of the early Church's prebaptismal instruction. Evidently that instruction was what, in the jargon of today, we should call thoroughly "existential." In other words, it was not so much "information" as "illumination." The biblical stories that played such an important part in it were not told—as "Bible stories" often are today, even by people who think that they are teaching religion—as more or less interesting bits of ancient history or folklore. They were given their conspicuous place in the program of basic Christian training because of the bright light they shed on the meaning of man's existence. They spoke of a transcendent destiny to which man is called by his Creator. They pointed to Christ, the Light of the world, as the guide to man's true destiny. They urged man to seek the "living water" which alone could sustain him on the way to his true destiny. To put it almost too simply, they summoned man to God, to Christ, to Baptism. They told of the eternal Light, which is God; of the Light of our world and our human time, which is Christ, the Son of God; of the sacramental moment of illumination, when the Light which is Christ shines in men's hearts. It is no exaggeration to say that such a witness to the Light is in itself an illumination of human life.

Earlier in this book I suggested that Lent and Easter are meant to be a corporate renewal of Baptism on the part of the whole Christian people. If we seriously intend to take part in that effort of renewal, what better guide can we find than the ancient Church's plan of preparation for Baptism? If we will only let them, the great stories of "The Water of Life," "The Light of the World," and "The Resurrection and the Life" will tell us once again what our life means, what Christ means for our life, and how Christ has entered our life to claim it for glory and for God.

CHAPTER 11

RESTORATION: PENITENCE

> O Jesu Christ, from thee began
> This healing for the soul of man,
> By fasting sought, by fasting found,
> Through forty days of yearly round;
>
> That he who fell from high delight,
> Borne down to sensual appetite,
> By dint of stern control may rise
> To climb the hills of Paradise.
>
> Therefore behold thy Church, O Lord,
> And grace of penitence accord
> To all who seek with generous tears
> Renewal of their wasted years.
>
> Forgive the sin that we have done,
> Forgive the course that we have run,
> And show henceforth in evil day
> Thyself our succour and our stay.
>
> But now let every heart prepare,
> By sacrifice of fast and prayer,
> To keep with joy magnifical
> The solemn Easter festival.
>   —Latin hymn, *ca.* ninth century

I am playing a word game with an alert young godson of mine. The idea is to see how quickly and appropriately he can match words that I throw at him. For five minutes he has kept the game moving at high speed, and he still shows no sign of slackening. "Queen," "club," "grapefruit," "white," and "train" follow "king," "golf," "oranges," "black," and "electric" without an instant's hesitation. It is time (I decide) to try something harder; this young man needs to be slowed down a bit. "Shrove Tuesday," I say, more or less at random. The boy does not falter. "Pancakes," he shouts triumphantly.

Despite certain professional reservations, I cannot seriously object to this response. Many people would probably have said the same thing, if they had said anything at all. Besides, my young friend is not old enough yet to know very much about the more important associations of Shrove Tuesday. Nonetheless, his answer does set me thinking how unfortunate it is that in so many minds the day before Lent stands for nothing more significant than a culinary specialty. If we do not see more in it than that, our Lent is off to a bad start.

Shrove Tuesday, as its name suggests, is traditionally a day for being "shriven." For many centuries, throughout a large part of Christendom, the most serious and devout Christians have made a point of going to confession and receiving absolution just before the beginning of Lent. The custom dates from the time when the Lenten discipline of the public penitents had begun to affect the Lenten observance of the whole Church, and it is fully in accordance with the meaning of Lent as an historic Christian institution. Lent is indeed a good deal more than a "penitential season," if by that we mean a time devoted to sorrow for our sins. Lent is the season of preparation for Easter. Lent is a time when we try to enter more deeply into Christ's sufferings as a preparation for sharing in his victory. But as we have seen, that experience of dying with Christ involves a constant dying to sin, and it is right that from start to finish our Lent should be filled with the spirit of penitence and marked by acts of penance.

Of course, many Christians do not practice confession in the particular form from which Shrove Tuesday takes its name. At least some readers of this book will belong to Christian communions which make little or no provision for private confession and question the idea of priestly absolution. Still others will be members of a church in which going to confession is a matter of personal conscience rather than of public rule. The issue is one on which Christendom has been more or less seriously divided for a long time. My own conviction is that "sacramental confession" is an important aid to Christian living; that every Christian can benefit from its use; and that in many cases, at any rate, it is essential to spiritual health. No doubt what I have to say about confession in general is influenced by this conviction and by the experience to which it has led me. I have no intention, however, of arguing here and now with those who conscientiously hold other views. What I do want is to bring out the lesson that the original meaning of Shrove Tuesday holds for every Christian who tries to keep Lent. That lesson is twofold. First, and more generally, if Lent is to be a time of intensive training in the Christian life, it must include exercise in penitence, because penitence is part of Christian living. Secondly, and more specifically, Lent must begin with confession, because penitence first expresses itself in the confession of sins. Whether we practice sacramental confession or not, we must make quite sure, as we enter on our Lenten observance, that we open our hearts to God in a full confession of our sins and an honest admission of our responsibility for them.

It is not hard to see why such explicit confession should be both the first and the chief act of penitence. There can be no repentance at all, no genuine sorrow for sin, no turning from sin and no growth into holiness, unless we see and admit what we have done; unless we recognize in our actions a denial of God's plan for human life; unless we acknowledge that God alone can restore us to our place in his plan. But when we faithfully and truly confess our sins, we do all these things together.

By bringing our sins to light in the act of confession, we fulfill the first condition of repentance. No doubt we can feel vaguely sinful without definite confession, but just feeling sinful is not real repentance, any more than just ceasing to feel sinful is a real experience of forgiveness. Our problem is not that we have caught some obscure disease called "sinfulness," which makes us uncomfortable. What is wrong with us is that we have deliberately committed certain acts called "sins," which have separated us from God. If our repentance is to be an effective restoration to fellowship with God, it cannot be a mere wallowing in dissatisfaction with ourselves. True repentance has to get at the real trouble, which is our sins. But that is exactly what happens when we bring out our sins in full and honest confession.

By confessing that the wrong actions which we have brought to light are a sin against God's purpose for man, we fulfill the second condition of repentance. No doubt we can be at least partially aware that certain acts are wrong, without explicitly recognizing them as sins against God, but such a limited awareness of the true character of our actions is an insufficient foundation for real repentance. For full and genuine repentance we need to see and acknowledge the enormity of our actions as sins against God himself—as a repeated rejection of the meaning that he intends our lives to have. What matters most in our sins is not the harm we do our neighbors or ourselves, but the rebellion against God's will and the separation from him which it entails. If our repentance is to be an effective restoration to fellowship with God, it cannot be a mere recognition that we have done wrong to ourselves or to any other finite beings. True repentance has to cut to the very root of our trouble and expose our sin as alienation from God. But that is exactly what happens when in the act of confessing our sins we acknowledge our sinful rebellion and ask God for pardon.

By asking God's forgiveness for the actions which we have recognized as sins against his purpose, we fulfill the third condition of repentance. No doubt we can do something about our sinful behavior without calling on God for pardon and aid, but to try to renew our lives without God is to fall far short of real repentance. Our sins are not just acts of cruelty or dishonesty or laziness or impurity or intemperance—human moral lapses which human moral effort can counteract. Our sins are acts of rebellion against God, and when we commit sin we break off our communion with him. But that communion which we throw away by disobedience is God's gift, and when it is lost God alone can restore it. If our repentance is to be an effective restoration to fellowship with God, it cannot be a mere human attempt at self-improve-

ment. True repentance must acknowledge man's ultimate help-
lessness and throw itself on God's mercy. But that is exactly what
happens when in confessing our sins to God we ask him to pardon
and renew us.

Let us suppose that our Lent has been duly begun with a full
examination of conscience and a solemn act of confession of our
sins. We have acknowledged our deliberate rejections of the moral
order; we have admitted that in rejecting the moral order we
were rebelling against the righteous Creator who established it;
we have asked God for the re-creating pardon which he alone
can give. What more must we do to carry out the penitential
purpose of Lent?

The answer lies in the nature of confession itself. When we set
about confessing our sins, we begin by looking back on them and
trying to see them for what they are. Then we spread out our sins
before God with sorrow, and ask him to pardon them for Jesus
Christ's sake. At first glance, that may appear to be all there is to
the act of confession—but in reality there is a good deal more.
What does genuine sorrow for sin involve? What does a sincere
prayer for pardon imply? Surely we are neither truly sorry for
sin nor honestly anxious for pardon unless we firmly purpose
amendment of life. We are not really sorry for an act that we
have half a mind to repeat; we do not care much for God's pardon if we are ready to betray it at the first opportunity.

It seems to follow that while confession of sin is the first and
chief act of penitence, it is something less than the whole story.
Confession itself implies the intention to amend our lives, and
amendment of life is something that we have to keep working at
all the time. We are constantly being tempted to relapse into sin,
and we must constantly be taking definite steps to fit ourselves for
the battle against temptation. In other words, we must try to
safeguard the stability of our repentance by doing what are often
called "works of penance."

Before we take a quick look at the Lenten works of penance,
we must guard ourselves against one crude misunderstanding of
their significance. Works of penance are neither a payment for

God's forgiveness nor a substitute for his continual help. Our restoration to the way of life is God's act of sheer grace, and without his constant aid we could not remain in that way for a moment. Works of penance, like all the other actions of Christian living, are acts of co-operation with God's grace, performed in accordance with St. Paul's injunction:

> . . . with reverence and awe make every effort to insure your salvation. . . . For it is God who in his good will is at work in your hearts, inspiring your will and your action.   Phil. 2:12–13

What distinguishes works of penance from other actions is simply the fact that they are done to discipline and strengthen believers for their Christian warfare against sin.

The traditional Christian works of penance are fasting, almsgiving, and prayer. Of course, all these actions are more than simply penitential in meaning, but they can readily be made to serve the purposes of penitence. How, after all, do we sin? We sin by using creatures irresponsibly and by letting their attraction seduce us from the love of God. But fasting, almsgiving, and prayer are exercises in the virtuous opposites of those fundamental vices—in the responsible use of creatures and in concentration on God. What better disciplines could we find, then, to train us away from sin? What clearer signs could we give of our aversion from sin and our purpose of amendment?

The same three traditional works of penance constitute the penitential discipline of Lent. The penitence of the whole Christian people in Lent does not differ substantially from the penitence of any Christian at any time. The purpose of the Lenten penitence is the purpose of all Christian penitence: the restoration of the sinner to fellowship with God. And the framework of the Lenten penitence is the ordinary framework of all Christian penitence: confession and the traditional works of penance. All that is as it should be, because Lent is a time of intensified Christian living, not an attempt at something radically different from the ordinary life of Christians.

Yet the penitential observance of Lent does have its own peculiar importance in the Christian scheme of things. The Lenten penitence brings out with unique clarity the ultimate meaning of all Christian penitence. In Lent, the Church's corporate penitence is drawn into her solemn preparation for the feast of the resurrection. In that setting, penitent Christians come closest to grasping the full significance of their repentance, because there they come closest to understanding the transcendent calling to which repentance restores them.

PART FOUR
VICTORS

CHAPTER 12

IMITATION: THE MARTYRS

The Son of God goes forth to war,
   A kingly crown to gain;
His blood-red banner streams afar!
   Who follows in his train?
Who best can drink his cup of woe,
   Triumphant over pain,
Who patient bears his cross below,
   He follows in his train.

The martyr first, whose eagle eye
   Could pierce beyond the grave;
Who saw his Master in the sky,
   And called on him to save.
Like him, with pardon on his tongue
   In midst of mortal pain,
He prayed for them that did the wrong!
   Who follows in his train?

A glorious band, the chosen few
   On whom the Spirit came,
Twelve valiant saints, their hope they knew,
   And mocked the cross and flame.
They met the tyrant's brandished steel,
   The lion's gory mane,
They bowed their necks the death to feel;
   Who follows in their train?

A noble army, men and boys,
   The matron and the maid,
Around the Saviour's throne rejoice
   In robes of light arrayed.
They climbed the steep ascent of heaven
   Through peril, toil, and pain;

O God, to us may grace be given
To follow in their train.
—Reginald Heber

Just a short time ago Jesus of Nazareth was arrested, tried, condemned, crucified, and buried. Thanks to some rather efficient police work, a very awkward episode in Roman-Jewish relations was thus ended. Yet his disciples are going about asserting that mankind has not heard the last of him—that on the contrary he "has taken his seat at God's right hand, from that time waiting for his enemies to be made his footstool" (Heb. 10:12–13). On the strength of this conviction, they have become quite aggressive, boldly declaring that in their Master's death and resurrection the hope of Israel has been fulfilled. The Messiah (they say) has come and the new age has dawned.

At least some of Jesus' followers are beginning to draw revolutionary conclusions from their basic claim. They are even arguing that the complex system of Jewish worship does not really matter any more. The rules of the Old Testament were only symbols of a reality that was still to come; now that the reality has come in Jesus Christ the old images have lost their importance. The born Jew who confesses Christ may still follow the old rules—insofar as they do not obstruct the union of Jews and Gentiles in the one Christ—from motives of piety or of loyalty to his people's great tradition. The Gentile Christian may interest himself in the events and the institutions of the Old Testament because to his mind they foreshadow God's definitive action in the Lord Jesus. But neither Jew nor Gentile can put any trust in the "old religion" as a way of salvation. The law of sacrifice and priesthood and temple has served its purpose and passed away, giving place to the eternal Gospel of Jesus Christ, in whom God's purpose is fully realized.

The religious authorities at Jerusalem are not pleased with what they hear of the new teaching. The priests who administer the Jerusalem temple, the great shrine of Judaism, are not generally thought to be the most devout and earnest members of the Jewish community, but there is no reason to suppose that they are not genuinely shocked by a frontal attack on the ancient ways of worship. In any case, altogether apart from the strictly religious issue, the political situation is tense, and it does not help to have religious strife break out, especially when such a notoriously explosive thing as a "Messianic" claim seems to be involved.

It is clear that something must be done, and done promptly. The authorities get hold of a particularly seditious Christian preacher named Stephen and bring him into court on a charge of blasphemy. Stephen responds with a speech which can only be called provocative.

> When they heard that, they were enraged and ground their teeth at him. But he, full of the holy Spirit, looked up to heaven and saw God's glory and Jesus standing at God's right hand. And he said,
>
> "Look! I can see heaven open, and the Son of Man standing at God's right hand!"
>
> But they uttered a great shout and stopped their ears, and they rushed upon him all together, and dragged him out of the city and stoned him, the witnesses throwing down their clothes at the feet of a young man named Saul. As they stoned Stephen, he prayed,
>
> "Lord Jesus, receive my spirit!"
>
> Then falling on his knees, he cried out,
>
> "Lord, do not lay this sin up against them!"
>
> With these words he fell asleep. Acts 7:54–60

Stephen, like his Master, has been safely disposed of. Yet in his way he too will continue to trouble the forces of law and order. His example will prove contagious, and following him an unending line of men and women, boys and girls, will boldly confess Christ without regard for earthly authority and the penalties it can inflict. By a wonderful irony, one of the first of the line will be the "young man named Saul," transformed from Saul the Pharisee into Paul the apostle to the Gentiles.

Through the centuries, St. Stephen and all those who have imitated him in a death for Christ's sake have been known to the Church as the "martyrs"—the incomparable "witnesses" to the Gospel of Jesus Christ. These are the believers who have taken that Gospel so seriously that they have been ready to die for it. These are the witnesses who have testified by real suffering and a real death to the real Gospel. Stephen the "Protomartyr" and the whole army of martyrs after him have borne their witness to God's mighty deed in Christ, not in speech or writing only, but in their own flesh and blood.

What stronger testimony could a man give to the crucified Lord than a death like his? How could his followers declare more forcefully that for them the Gospel of Christ is the key to the human mystery of life and death? In dying for Christ, the martyrs have become his privileged witnesses. But that is not all. According to the great tradition of Christendom, the martyrs are to be honored as privileged participants in Christ's sufferings. Of course, every Christian both can and must offer up his own suffering and death to God in union with the crucified Christ. But the martyr has a peculiar and significant privilege. His union with Christ in death extends even to outward circumstances, since like his Lord and Savior he dies at the hands of the enemies of God's truth.

The early Christian imagination loved to dwell on the similarities between the deaths of individual martyrs and the death of Christ himself. Ancient Christian literature, including the New Testament, contains many expressions of this interest. In Luke-Acts, for example, the passion of Christ and the martyrdom of Stephen are reported in such a way that their resemblance cannot be missed. The classical "Acts of the Martyrs," beginning with the second-century *Martyrdom of Polycarp*, consistently tell the same kind of story, more or less explicitly. The sermons preached by the Church fathers on the festivals of martyrs repeatedly point out the likeness between the sufferings of Christ and the sufferings endured by the martyrs in his name. It is quite evident that the idea of the martyr as the privileged imitator of the crucified Lord is deeply rooted in the Christian tradition.

The point is that in the call to imitate Christ in death the martyr's discipleship is visibly approved and sealed. Like the Lord Christ himself, to the naked eye the martyr is a failure. His death is nothing more than a last futile gesture—the predictable end of a life obsessed by an imaginary ideal. To the eye of faith, on the other hand, the martyr's death, like Christ's own death, is a prelude to final and total victory. If the martyr dies with Christ, he will also live with him. The invitation to share so completely in Christ's sufferings is nothing less than a tangible pledge of triumph. An old Greek hymn gives vivid expression to this Christian estimate of martyrdom:

> Let our choir new anthems raise,
>   Wake the morn with gladness;
> God himself to joy and praise
>   Turns the martyrs' sadness:
> This the day that won their crown,
>   Opened heaven's bright portal,
> As they laid the mortal down
>   And put on the immortal.
>
> Faith they had that knew no shame,
>   Love that could not languish;
> And eternal hope o'ercame
>   Momentary anguish.
> He who trod the selfsame road
>   Death and hell defeated;
> Wherefore these their passions showed
>   Calvary repeated.

If we supposed that death was the termination of human existence, we should be unlikely to celebrate the anniversary of a man's death as a festival. Birthdays and marriage anniversaries would still be suitable occasions for a joyful celebration, but the destruction of a man by death could only be mourned, or at best accepted. But because the Church linked martyrdom so closely to Christ's victorious death, she began very early to keep the anniversaries of her martyrs' deaths as solemn festivals. "Almighty and everlasting God, who hast consecrated the bright and holy joy of this day by the solemnity of thy blessed martyr. . . ."— so an old and typical prayer begins. As the centuries passed, the round of martyrs' festivals became almost a second Christian year, superimposed on the Sunday-and-Easter cycle of celebrations.

To the casual observer the Church may seem to have made a

false move in allowing this new Christian year to develop. Both in its content and in its form the new cycle of feasts looks quite different from the original Christian calendar. The holy days and seasons of the basic Christian year were designed to proclaim God's own mighty acts within human history. In sharp contrast, these new holy days are apparently kept in honor of mere human beings. The old calendar, shaped by the weekly commemoration and the annual celebration of God's redemptive acts, is orderly and logical. The new calendar is something else again; its holy days, corresponding as closely as possible to the actual dates of death of a number of individuals, fall haphazardly through the year. Apart from the fact that they both fit somehow into the developed pattern of Christian worship, the two cycles appear to have little or nothing in common.

Yet a little study will show that in reality they have a good deal in common. In a sense, the "second Christian year" is the completion of the first. If the Christian year of the Gospel announces what God has done in Christ for mankind, the Christian year of the martyrs tells how this new creation has taken effect in the lives and the deaths of the heroes of faith. Even the superficially random organization of the second Christian year really secures its close connection with the fundamental Christian calendar. The heart of the Christian year of the Gospel is the Paschal celebration of Christ's triumph; the very essence of the Christian year of the martyrs is the repeated remembrance of the victorious death of believers in Christ. In short, the second Christian year completes the first by celebrating the participation of Christians in the victory gained once for all by Christ himself.

No doubt (we may say) all that is very fine, but what does it have to do with us? It is instructive to learn that the feasts of the martyrs are really a swarm of little "Paschas" surrounding the great "Pascha"—the celebration of Christ's death and resurrection—but it is still not clear how that fact brings victory in Christ any closer for us. We may be quite ready to give the martyrs their due, but somehow they still seem remote from us. If and when we think about our own death, it is not a martyr's death that we ordinarily anticipate. Sudden obliteration in an airplane crash, incineration in a nuclear war, the lingering death of cancer, the shock and pain of a heart attack—these, rather than being thrown to the lions or burned at the stake, are the images of death that are likely to cross our minds. To most of us, the various forms of Christian martyrdom seem to belong to a picturesque and vanished past, and we pay little attention to them in our calculations regarding our own future. Under these circumstances, what can the story of the martyrs say to us?

The answer must be that Christian martyrdom speaks to us all of our common destiny as believers in Christ. The way of martyrdom is one particular way to a common goal. If it is true (as historic Christianity maintains) that the martyr's calling is a special gift of God's grace, summoning the believer to eternal life by the same path that Christ trod, it is no less true that all believers are called to the same destiny. The martyr may be the Christian whose discipleship has been visibly completed and sealed, but he is far from being the only full Christian. On the contrary, he is a sign to all Christians of their common hope.

In the first great age of the martyrs, when Christianity and pagan culture met in a life-and-death struggle, the Church's outstanding teachers and pastors did their best to keep the whole truth in view. They would neither conceal the glory of martyrdom nor suggest that it was the one truly Christian way to die. On the one hand, they tried to prepare their flocks to face death for Christ's sake if the call should come; on the other hand, they worked hard to discourage believers from rushing madly into martyrdom as if it were the universal vocation of genuine Christians.

As time went on, the Church showed her regard for other ways of Christian living and dying by expanding the Christian year of the martyrs into the Christian year of all saints. In the Church's eyes, heroic virtue, as well as heroic death, was a true witness to the Gospel of redemption, and the holy death that sealed a holy life might be as much a "Paschal" event as martyrdom itself. Other Christians as well as the martyrs could imitate Christ in the sacrificial offering of obedience to God, culminating in the courageous acceptance of death, and their deaths too could be celebrated as a passage in Christ from time to eternity. In the fully developed Christian year, the martyrs would still be honored as unique signs of God's power, but the effectual presence of the same power in all God's saints would be explicitly and fully acknowledged.

It is the whole story, then, of God's triumph in his saints that the Church celebrates in the second Christian year. And she carries out that celebration for the sake of us all, to draw us more fully into the Christian mystery of death and resurrection. When we are summoned to celebrate the deaths of the saints, we are invited at once to confess and to deepen our own conviction that for believers in the triumphant Christ death is the opened gate to eternal life.

CHAPTER 13

THANKS BE TO GOD!

Jesus lives! thy terrors now
   Can, O death, no more appal us;
Jesus lives! by this we know
   Thou, O grave, canst not enthral us.
               Alleluia!

Jesus lives! henceforth is death
   But the gate of life immortal;
This shall calm our trembling breath,
   When we pass its gloomy portal.
               Alleluia!

Jesus lives! for us he died;
   Then, alone to Jesus living,
Pure in heart may we abide,
   Glory to our Saviour giving.
               Alleluia!

Jesus lives! our hearts know well
   Nought from us his love shall sever;
Life, nor death, nor powers of hell
   Tear us from his keeping ever.
               Alleluia!
            —Christian Gellert

Jesus Christ has conquered. In his death and resurrection the incarnate Son of God has triumphed over death and won his way to the destiny for which mankind was made. The ultimate meaning of man's existence has been realized, and the threat of ultimate meaninglessness has been disposed of once and for all. In fact, the very event that denied absolute and enduring meaning to human life has become the gateway to man's eternal fulfillment. By dying and rising to life again, the victorious Lord has transformed death itself.

The victory of Jesus Christ is a victory for the whole race of men, and every child of man can claim it for his own. Christ died to free men from sin and rose from the dead to bring them to their true destiny in God. In the divine purpose for our world, the Good Shepherd and his ransomed flock belong together.

Through his Church the risen Saviour is constantly calling men and women and little children to share in his triumph over death and over the sin that enslaves us to death. In the sacraments of the Gospel he shows forth his victory and communicates its benefits. Week by week on the Lord's Day, and year by year on the "Feast of feasts," he invites us to recall and to celebrate the events in which his victory was won. In the martyrs and saints, the great victors of faith, he offers us all a glorious pledge of the hope of our calling.

Jesus Christ has conquered. Jesus Christ announces his victory in the sacraments of his Gospel, in the worship of his Church, in the righteousness of his saints. There, roughly outlined, is the story of Christ and his Church. But that story is not a tidily finished tale that we can read with relaxed enjoyment. On the contrary, each of us is expected to contribute his own chapter, written on his own mind and heart, flesh and blood. If God's will is to be fully done, each of us must have the story of his own victory in Christ to tell.

The conflict with sin and death is the one battle from which no man can ever be exempted. Every human being is born into a world corrupted by sin and given over to death. Every human being has to make repeated moral choices in the face of insistent temptation. Every human being is destined to die. We are not asked whether we enjoy making moral decisions in a sin-distorted world, or whether we really want to die; we have to decide and we have to die. The battle is inescapable, and the Christian faith holds out no false hope of peace. What it does tell us is that God's mercy has provided a real alternative to defeat. Thanks to his gracious action in Jesus Christ, we can choose good rather than evil, eternal life rather than eternal death.

"Thank God! He gives us victory through our Lord Jesus Christ" (1 Cor. 15:57). God has won the victory over sin and death, and now each of us can make his own life and death a fresh chapter in the story of divine triumph. All that is required is that we should respond with all our heart and strength to God's powerful summons to victory.

"Thank God! He gives us victory through our Lord Jesus Christ." If that is true of our own living and dying, then in the long run nothing else matters. The conflict with sin may be grim and wearisome, and the suffering and tragedy that beset us may seem overwhelming. But if we remain faithful and steadfast in our baptismal union with Christ amid toil and tribulation and tumult, we shall be more than conquerors in him.

"Thank God! He gives us victory through our Lord Jesus Christ." As I write these closing lines, the threat of war hangs darkly over Germany and the world. I must frankly admit that my mind sometimes wanders and I find myself looking with a shocked incredulity at the madness of a fallen world or (more self-centeredly) wondering whether the words I am now putting on paper will ever appear in print to speak to other men's minds. But I am soon drawn back to my task, because what I am writing about is nothing less than God's final answer to human sin and human suffering. God's bright and beautiful creation may be devastated and God's children may suffer incalculable harm through the culpable stupidity or the sheer malice of men. But God has already spoken the last word on human history, and that word is a message of ultimate hope. The defeat of earthly hopes and the frustration of human purposes are small things beside the glory that has been disclosed in the death and resurrection of Jesus Christ.

"Thank God! He gives us victory through our Lord Jesus Christ." In the midst of sin and pain and death, the Church lifts up her heart in grateful adoration. Christ has overcome the sharpness of death and opened the kingdom of heaven to all believers, and Christians cannot be sorrowful, as if they had no hope. Their hearts are fixed on their crucified and risen Lord, and they summon the world to acknowledge his triumph.

> Crown him the Lord of life,
> Who triumphed o'er the grave,
> And rose victorious in the strife
> For those he came to save.
> His glories now we sing
> Who died and rose on high,
> Who died eternal life to bring,
> And lives that death may die.

SOURCES*

PAGE LINE†

17 1 Henry Vaughan, "Departed Friends."
18 19 Herman Feifel, in *The Meaning of Death* (New York, 1959), p. xiii.
18 24 Charles Péguy, *Temporal and Eternal* (New York, 1958), pp. 141–42.
19 23 Corliss Lamont, *The Illusion of Immortality,* 3rd ed. (New York, 1959), p. 73.
20 25 *Ibid.,* p. 182.
22 25 Willa Cather, *Obscure Destinies* (New York, 1932), p. 73.
24 21 Corliss Lamont, *op. cit.,* p. 258.
30 30 George Santayana, *Reason in Religion* (New York, 1926), p. 240.
32 23 Jaroslav Pelikan, *The Shape of Death* (Nashville, 1961), p. 23.
33 29 Bede, *Church History of the English Nation,* Bk. II, chap. 13.
34 19 Corliss Lamont, *op. cit.,* p. 3.
34 26 Cf. *The Globe and Mail,* Toronto, May 13, 1961, p. 44.
37 1 Latin sequence, *Victimae paschali,* opening lines.
40 3 "Death's mightiest powers": from Latin hymn (probably eighteenth century), *Finita iam sunt proelia.*
40 7 "He is risen"; first stanza of hymn by Cecil F. Alexander.
40 21 Fortunatus, "Sing, my tongue": *Pange, lingua, gloriosi proelium certaminis,* first stanza.
40 27 Fortunatus, "Abroad the regal banners": *Vexilla regis prodeunt,* first stanza.
44 32 Cecil F. Alexander, "There Is a Green Hill Far Away."
53 1 St. John of Damascus, "Come, ye faithful": ode from the "Canon for St. Thomas' Sunday" (First Sunday after Easter), first stanza.
71 1 "With Christ we share": first two stanzas of a carol from Neale's *Carols for Christmas and Eastertide* (1853).

* Most translations of Latin and Greek hymns are from J. M. Neale (sometimes revised). Translation on p. 120 is by M. F. Bell, and translations on pp. 123 and 135 are by T. A. Lacey. These are from *The English Hymnal* (1906, rev. 1933).

† The number given indicates the beginning line of each quotation.

PAGE	LINE	
76	22	Louis Beirnaert, S.J., in *La Maison-Dieu,* No. 22 (1950, 3rd quarter), pp. 95 f.
82	3	Charles Wesley, "A Charge to Keep I Have."
83	1	"The Lamb's high banquet": first four stanzas of Latin hymn, *Ad coenam agni providi.*
91	15	"Paschal Lamb, thine offering": from hymn by George H. Bourne, beginning "Lord, enthroned in heavenly splendour."
94	19	"Types and shadows": from Aquinas' "Vespers Hymn for Corpus Christi," beginning *Pange, lingua, gloriosi corporis mysterium.*
95	1	Aquinas, "Lo! the new King's table," and "Lo! the angels' food" (line 6): from the sequence for "Corpus Christi" beginning *Lauda, Sion, salvatorem.*
95	32	St. Cyprian, *Epistle* 63.
96	14	"We offer to thee": from hymn by V. S. S. Coles beginning "Almighty Father, Lord most high."
98	31	"Salvation's Giver": from Irish hymn, probably seventh century, beginning "Draw nigh and take the body of the Lord." First line of original: *Sancti, venite, corpus Christi sumite.* Text from *The Bangor Antiphonary* (late seventh century).
103	1	"This is the day": from Watts's *Psalms of David* (1719), paraphrase of Ps. 118 entitled "Hosanna: the Lord's Day."
109	1	" 'Tis the spring": first stanza of ode from the "Canon for St. Thomas' Sunday" (First Sunday after Easter) by St. John of Damascus.
114	1	"Alleluia we deserve not": from "Alleluia! song of sweetness." Original first line: *Alleluia, dulce carmen.*
116	20	St. Leo, *Sermon* 45, 1.
120	1	"The glory of these forty days": first and following stanzas of hymn, *Clarum decus ieiunii.*
123	11	"Give us the self-control": from "O kind Creator, bow thine ear," ascribed to St. Gregory the Great. Original first line: *Audi, benigne conditor.*
127	1	"Christ, whose glory": This is the entire hymn by Charles Wesley.
135	1	"O Jesu Christ": first five stanzas of hymn *Jesu quadragenariae.*
145	1	"The Son of God goes forth to war": "Hymn for St. Stephen's Day" by Reginald Heber.
149	7	"Let our choir new anthems raise": from the "Canon for St. Timothy and St. Maura" by St. Joseph the Hymnographer.

PAGE   LINE

153   1   "Jesus lives!": first four stanzas of hymn, *Jesus lebt, mit ihm auch ich* by Christian Gellert.

156   5   "Crown him the Lord of life": from Godfrey Thring's additions to Matthew Bridges' hymn, "Crown him with many crowns."